Current Trends in Secondary
School Social Studies

THE PROFESSIONAL EDUCATION SERIES

Walter K. Beggs, *Editor*
Dean Emeritus, Teachers College, and
Professor of Educational Administration
University of Nebraska

Royce H. Knapp, *Research Editor*
Regents Professor of Education
University of Nebraska

Current Trends in Secondary School Social Studies

by

RANDALL C. ANDERSON

Professor of Social Sciences
Kansas State Teachers College

PROFESSIONAL EDUCATORS PUBLICATIONS, INC.
LINCOLN, NEBRASKA

Material on pages 59-70 originally published under the title "Introducing the World Population Crises to Secondary Social Studies Classes: An Inquiry-Oriented Instructional Strategy," by Randall C. Anderson, *Social Education,* Vol. 34, No. 1 (January, 1970). By permission of the National Council for the Social Studies.

Material on pages 83-92 originally published under the title "The Role of Human Geography in the Study of Emerging Nations," by R. C. Anderson, *Social Education,* Vol. 29, No. 6 (October, 1965). By permission of the National Council for the Social Studies.

Library of Congress Catalog Card No.: 72-77984

ISBN   0-88224-001-3

Contents

Preface

This book was prepared for prospective secondary social studies teachers, in-service teachers, educational administrators, professors of social studies education, and members of the public who are interested and concerned about the social studies as a major component of the secondary school program. Professionally, the book is designed for use in secondary social studies methods courses at both the undergraduate and graduate levels.

The substantive portion of the book, Chapters 3 and 4, attempts to reflect the most futuristic thinking in social studies curriculum planning—that of designing a curriculum which incorporates the study of major interdisciplinary themes involving the human and social condition. The secondary social studies curriculum comprises subject matter selected from the following seven distinct disciplines: history, geography, political science, economics, sociology, anthropology, and social psychology. Since World War II, the traditional social science disciplines of history, geography, and government have been challenged by the newer behaviorally oriented areas of sociology, anthropology, and social psychology for a more significant role in the secondary curriculum. The impossibility of significantly expanding the secondary curriculum to include a separate course representing each of the social and behavioral sciences has encouraged many leaders in social education to propose various innovative strategies for the social studies curriculum which will integrate effectively the basic materials and concepts from the various subject matter areas. One approach which has received a great deal of support is the development of a secondary social studies program around selected contemporary domestic and international themes. Such a technique would place emphasis upon the interdisciplinary nature of the various cultural, economic, and political issues confronting society as well as making the secondary social studies curriculum more relevant for American youth. Such is the curricular approach suggested by this book.

The writer is particularly grateful to Dr. Royce H. Knapp, Regents Professor of History and Philosophy of Education, University of Nebraska, and to Dr. William H. Seiler, Chairman of the Division of Social Sciences, The Kansas State Teachers College of Emporia, for their inspiration and guidance in the preparation of this book. The author also wishes to acknowledge Miss Linda Attig and Jana Justiz for their untiring assistance in the preparation and typing of the manuscript.

CHAPTER 1

The Changing Rationale for Social Studies Instruction

DEFINING THE SOCIAL SCIENCE DISCIPLINES AND THE SOCIAL STUDIES

A social science discipline is a field of study. Thus, it is an organized body of information with a particular methodology or mode of inquiry. The area or field of study refers to the data or information studied, the method of collecting information, and the questions asked by scholars representing the disciplines. Thus, each of the social science disciplines consists of an organized body of knowledge. However, this body of knowledge consists of much more than an agglomeration of descriptive facts. Indeed, unless facts are grouped together resulting in relationships, they are of little value in explaining issues and events. Facts in each of the social science disciplines are classified under headings referred to as concepts. Groups of concepts, for instance, may be related to offer historical or political explanations of past or current events. The structure of a field or discipline refers to the way in which facts and concepts are interrelated.[1]

Each social science discipline possesses a unique methodology or mode of inquiry. The method may be that of statistical correlation such as in the field of psychology, the historical method based upon positive or negative affirmation of documentary evidence as in history, that of empiricism as in the sciences, or logic as in mathematics. Each of the disciplines comprising the social sciences has developed a particular method and set of procedures to accomplish its search for data, facts, and the development of concepts. Each of the social sciences, for example, anthropology, economics, geography, history, political science, sociology, and social psychology, is a subject matter area which deals with the human condition, human relationships, human behavior, and human-environmental relationships. Although a number of the social sciences use some research techniques in common, each subject area is prone to develop specialized techniques because of the type of human information studied and questions asked.[2]

As a result of the application of these research or inquiry techniques, the social science disciplines are changing constantly. The change is continued as new information is accumulated within the field, giving rise to new areas of inquiry. For instance, the sociologist analyzes a new social movement or developing mores. An anthropologist examines different cultural characteristics. Geographers examine changes in particular regions through time and environmental impact. The historian studies contemporary events in light of past events, while the political scientist analyzes political behavior patterns and the economist the economy of underdeveloped nations.[3]

In recent years the change among the social sciences has been most rapid. Political science has been revolutionized by a change in the type of questions asked. Sociologists have developed new theories to guide their research and synthesize their knowledge. National income statistics and econometrics, by providing new techniques of analysis, have enabled economists to improve their explanatory and predictive ability. Similarly, geographers have developed new statistical techniques and new mapping techniques. New procedures in analyzing historical data have resulted in new historical interpretations. Anthropologists have widened their studies to include the study of non-primitive cultures.[4] There are only a few indications of the changes which have taken place, changes which have outmoded much that is currently being taught in the junior and senior high social sciences.

Relationships Among the Social Science Disciplines and the Secondary Curriculum

Some scholars representing the various social science disciplines believe that the several social science subject areas could be integrated into one basic science concerning the study of human behavioral patterns. Thus far, at the collegiate level, however, attempts to integrate the various subject areas have proved largely unsuccessful, although there is now some evidence that this traditional situation is changing. Nevertheless, the social sciences have much in common and complement one another in many respects. Thus, they do form an integrated area of study. Scholars and teachers in each of the social science disciplines are all concerned with human, cultural, and social research and information, and in many instances, similar aspects of the same human phenomena.[5]

The secondary school social science curriculum cannot possibly incorporate all of the research materials which have been organized in each of the social science disciplines. Obviously, there is not the classroom time for students to become acquainted with all of these topics even in an artificial fashion. Thus, the question of priority concerning content selection from all of the social science disciplines continues to be debated.

Defining the Secondary Social Studies

The relationship between the social studies in the secondary curriculum and the academic social sciences is many times confusing to students in teacher education programs as well as individuals unacquainted with the literature of professional education. However, controversies involving the recognized distinctions between the terms social sciences and social studies are quite irrelevant to the conscientious thought that is currently being given to the consideration of what new strategies to implement in the secondary curriculum.

As noted above, the social science disciplines are separate areas of organized academic fields of study whose content is organized around social, cultural, and human relationships and behavior. Each of the social sciences possesses a method of research or inquiry to continually investigate human and social phenomena and, thus, create new knowledge for the various disciplines. The investigators and practitioners of this new knowledge are usually associated with the academic departments of colleges and universities or some other research organization.[6]

The social studies in the secondary school curriculum are distinguishable from the social science disciplines in the following four basic respects: (1) scope, (2) size, (3) purpose, and (4) level of difficulty. In both scope and size the social sciences are much more extensive than the social studies.[7] Scholars representing the various social science disciplines research a greater diversity of social and human relationships and gather considerably more data and information than it is conceivably possible to include in the secondary social studies program. The purpose of the social scientist is to search and contribute new knowledge to his discipline. The objective of the secondary social studies teacher is to direct students in their learning of selected segments of what the social scientists have discovered. Social studies material draws upon the literature of the social sciences, but its purpose is not to report the discovery of new research. In their research social scientists deal frequently with abstract theories and sophisticated modes of inquiry that, in most instances, are beyond the comprehension of many secondary students. The social studies instructor, therefore, selects content based upon the research of social scientists and develops innovative techniques for translating it into comprehensible materials for the secondary student. Thus, there exists no absolute delimitation between the social sciences and the social studies. Rather, there is a difference in methodology and application.

Defining the Secondary Social Studies Subject Areas

Anthropology. Anthropology in secondary education is the study of different ethnic and racial groups, languages, and cultural traditions existing in various global regions in different historical periods. The emphasis of anthropological study at the secondary level should be the analysis and explanation of why world cultures differ from one another.

Economics. Although the study of economics is highly theoretical in higher education, its major emphasis in the secondary social studies should be upon man's continued attempt to satisfy his material needs. Economics instruction introduces students to the production and allocation of capital, private business, large corporations, tax structures, stocks and bonds, and the economic structure of agriculture and government. In addition to studying the financial structure of the various private and governmental economic sectors, secondary school economics should prepare students to manage their personal financial responsibilities.

Geography. The predominant view among many social studies instructors is that geography is a descriptive subject, quite similar to geology, with the primary purpose of providing a static environmental base for historical, political, economic, and sociological study. On the contrary, for secondary school purposes, geography should be a dynamic study of man's acquired behavioral patterns and his technological impact upon both the natural and cultural environment. As such, geography must be related to the political, economic, and cultural processes in particular areas in order to show the interaction between geographic phenomena and other aspects of socially controlled behavior.

History. History continues to be a major component of the secondary school curriculum even though many professional historians and educators feel that it should be defined as one of the humanities rather than as a social and behavioral study. History, as a component of the social studies should be a study of man's recorded past. Similar to the basic problem confronting geography, history should not be a consideration of disconnected dates and events but, rather, it should be an interpretative consideration of the physical, human, economic, and social forces that have shaped past events and institutions. A methodological emphasis at the secondary level should be to acquaint students with the significance of original or primary sources and with the problems associated with the determination of the validity of evidence used in the reconstruction of the past.

Political Science. This subject area should acquaint students with local, state, federal, and international governing bodies. One major theme should be to examine the relationships that exist between the federal, state, and local governments in the United States. A second theme should be the comparative study of governments, with emphasis placed upon the differences existing between totalitarian and democratic governments. Third, students should be aware of the problems, prospects, and operative structure of international political agencies, such as the United Nations.

Social Psychology. This subject should prepare students to better comprehend the forces which contribute to the behavioral patterns of individuals and groups. Thus, both the psychological and physiological aspects of personal and societal behavioral and motivational traits should be incorporated into any consideration of social psychology.

Sociology. Closely related to both anthropology and social psychology is the rapidly expanding subject area of sociology. The content of sociology is upon culture and society, with emphasis placed upon the study of the various types of interaction and relationships which exist among individuals and human groups. In the study of social organization and disorganization, sociologists attempt to explain the evolution and change of social institutions and the changing nature of human attitudinal and value systems. Thus, the changing nature of family life, institutional life, sexual attitudes, crime, religious values, and the interpersonal relationships in politics and government are among the topics included within the study of sociology.

These subject areas comprise the major elements of the secondary social studies curriculum. The traditional subjects of history, geography, and government will continue to be challenged by the newer areas of anthropology, sociology, and social psychology, which emphasize the consideration of human behavioral patterns.

Nevertheless, the subject fields will continue to contain a significant proportion of integrated material, regardless of the specific name attached to the course. In the near future it will probably become increasingly difficult to measure a subject's status on the basis of separate and required offerings in the secondary social studies curriculum. The expanding "crush" of knowledge renders this situation inevitable. Integration or correlation of content implies no sacrifice of academic purity. On the contrary, such an approach is the only possible means to acquaint secondary students with the content and methods of each of the social science disciplines.

EMERGING INTERPRETATIONS OF EDUCATION FOR DEMOCRATIC CITIZENSHIP

The claim that the foremost objective of the American system of precollegiate public education is the development of good citizens for a democratic society is probably one of the most frequently stated goals in the professional literature. This educational "fact" has most significant implications for the secondary school social studies curriculum. Obviously, citizenship values are claimed for all areas of the secondary curriculum. However, of all the subject areas comprising the secondary curriculum, the social studies program is the field most directly responsible for the transmission of those values, ideals, and elements of the cultural heritage to the nation's youth with the ultimate objective of producing "democratic citizens." Thus, the social studies program is more directly responsible for the development and perpetuation of strong feelings of loyalty and patriotism among the nation's inhabitants and, hence, a high degree of national viability and cohesion than any other subject matter area. The inculcation of citizenship education based upon a high degree of nationalism among the populace will continue to be the ultimate rationale for social education in the secondary school.

Modern Definitions of Citizenship Education

Controversies concerning the role of education in a democracy during recent years have directly or indirectly involved the issue of the responsibility of the nation's schools in transmitting the nation's cultural heritage and nationalistic ideals. There are those segments of society which blamed the schools and especially the social studies curriculum for every "unpatriotic" characteristic[8] they believe to be increasing in American society.

The curricular programs suggested for preparing effective citizens of a democratic society have ranged all the way from "life adjustment" curricula to programs based upon traditional spiritual and moral training. For instance, foreign language teachers claim their courses promote the type of cross-cultural understanding essential to the acquisition of good citizenship characteristics. Teachers of more utilitarian subjects such as business and industrial arts subjects argue that the inclusion of vocational training in the secondary curriculum is vital to citizenship development, since students who have achieved salable skills are individuals who are unlikely to become burdens on society, and, thus, good citizens. Many educators have noted the positive correlation between emotional adjustment and citizenship behavior. Emotionally ill or maladjusted individuals are more prone to develop antisocial and unlawful behavioral patterns than well-adjusted people. Obviously, this multiplicity of curricular approaches suggested for the development of a "democratic" citizen is highly confusing to teachers and the public.[9] The amorphous nature of the curricular approaches advanced in the name of citizenship education often results in a loss of meaning or significance of the term itself among teachers and educators.

Significantly, however, this confusion did not begin as a result of debates among educators. The essence of the argument has its foundation in the nebulousness of the English language and, as a result, several distinctly different interpretations of the term "citizenship" have evolved and will continue to evolve, particularly in the literature of the secondary social studies.

Citizenship Education and the Social Order

One widely professional as well as public definition of democratic citizenship is that which is referred to as worthy membership in American society.[10] According to this view, an individual's activities as a producer and consumer, his worthy membership in social and cultural groups, the manner in which he respects or fails to respect public and private property, and even the way in which he raises his children have significant implications for the community in which he lives. Thus, any curriculum which contributes to the physical, emotional, social, or moral development of youth contributes directly to the welfare of the community and should be considered as education for democratic citizenship.[11] This thesis holds that citizenship education is indistinguishable from social studies education or general education.

Citizenship Education and Political Socialization

A second view of education for democratic citizenship is much more specific in its definition. This is that citizenship is a political role; it is based upon actual participation in a democratic state. For those who expound this view, citizenship education is education for competency in participation in our modern democratic society. Specifically, a democratic populace must comprehend and appreciate the political character of their society, its goals and objectives, its limitations, its methods of operation, and the boundaries of reasonable choice in their nation and in the international community. Every nation requires a human resource with certain types of knowledge and particular skills, but if a democratic nation is to continue to exist, its citizens must have a knowledgeable understanding of their political system and how it functions. Obviously, the basic objectives are to perpetuate our cultural heritage, thus promoting patriotism and national viability and cohesion and instilling strong nationalistic feelings concerning American values and ideals. As a result, the citizenry within a democracy plan an active role in public affairs — community, state, and national. Indeed, in many instances the efforts of the people determines national policy. Thus, they must be acquainted with the political action.[12]

This second definition explicitly implies that the social studies curriculum is much more directly responsible for citizenship education than any other curricular area. Many secondary social studies teachers are thoroughly convinced that this is such a significant objective that they wish to base the entire social studies curriculum on the rationale of education for democratic citizenship. This philosophy assumes that all citizens have an important role to play in our democracy. Indeed, if citizens do not fulfill their political responsibilities intelligently, or if they remain apathetic to the democratic process, the nation itself will fail to achieve its democratic responsibilities. Such a state of affairs would eventually result in the erosion and destruction of one of the fundamental values of our society.

Citizenship, Education, and Political Dissent

A rapidly emerging rationale for the secondary social studies curriculum is that it should prepare and equip students with the knowledge and ability to take an overt part in political activities in order to facilitate human, social, and economic change within our ever-evolving democratic society. This view of the ultimate objective of social studies in secondary education is based upon the hypothesis that our society has been, is, and will continue to be beset by many social, political, and economic problems which challenge many of our other values and that the people must be allowed to exert considerable influence in attempting to solve these problems. In essence, it is the responsibility of all citizens to actively participate in bringing about change in the nation's social, economic, and political institutions; changes which have and will continue to become necessary, since many traditional institutions will not function adequately in a cultural and natural environment characterized by rapid technological change. Therefore, the secondary social studies curriculum should prepare American youth to adjust to the social change taking place about them, but also to participate actively in directing and implementing economic, social, and political change through community, state, and federal political institutions.

There exist two unique characteristics regarding this third definition of citizenship education with respect to the first two views noted above. First, the latter philosophy places more priority upon utilizing subject matter from the social science disciplines in the secondary curriculum. Secondary social studies teachers who expound this third definition argue that other curricular fields contribute to citizenship education but they consider the social studies program as the foremost curricular agent and, thus, primary responsibility for the political socialization or citizenship training of the nation's youth. In essence, training for democratic citizenship is the domain of the social studies curriculum in secondary education.

The second and equally significant characteristic of the third philosophy of citizenship education is that the social studies curriculum should prepare and actively encourage students to become involved in social change through engaging in political dissent within the broad limits of the democratic process. To a great extent, this rationale challenges the traditional philosophy that the social studies must act as the curricular agent for the transmission of our cultural heritage for the purpose of emphasizing only the positive aspects of the nation's historical, political, and social development, and thus, a high degree of national cohesion and unity. Indeed, this latter view would encourage students to become aware of the inconsistencies, inequalities, and inequities which have characterized the nation's evolution and which continue to exist within American society so that they will be adequately prepared to take part in resolving these obvious negative characteristics through active participation in the various social "movements" which are based upon dissent against the traditional, cultural, and social institutions within society. This increasing number of educators base their rationale for such a social studies curriculum upon the definition of a democratic citizen whose foremost responsibility is one of protecting an interpretation of the basic freedoms which must exist within a democratic society (for example, the freedoms of speech, press, petition, and assembly).

Through social studies instruction students should achieve the understanding that the function of freedom, both domestic and international, is not merely to protect and exalt the individual — vital as that is to the health of society. Furthermore, we must foster freedom in order to avoid error and discover truth; so far there has been no other means found to achieve this objective. The same is true with conscientious dissents. Students should understand that dissent is not to be indulged in for sentimental or selfish reasons. Rather, students should be encouraged to dissent because our concept of democratic freedom is dependent upon it.[13]

This concept of the secondary social science curriculum accepts the basic orientation of professional educators toward curriculum planning: that objectives for social studies instruction can be specified in some detail under the general headings of knowledge or understandings, skills, and attitudes. However, they proceed to enumerate these objects and skills in terms of preparing youth to comprehend the nature of controversial societal issues and thereby actively participate in formulating economic, political, and social change which is so vital to preserving and improving our system of democracy.

BEHAVIORAL CHANGE AS AN OBJECTIVE OF SOCIAL EDUCATION

Curriculum planning in social studies education is commonly considered in terms of the following major categories:[14]

1. What educational purposes or objectives should the course seek to achieve?
2. What learning experiences can be provided that are likely to bring about the realization of these purposes?
3. How can these learning experiences be effectively organized to help provide scope and sequence for the learner and to help the student in integrating what might otherwise appear as isolated learning experiences?
4. How can the effectiveness of learning experiences be evaluated by the use of tests and other systematic evidence-gathering procedures?

The significance of analyzing these four major goals involves the extent to which they will contribute to influencing student change through the educative process. In other words, the ways in which these objectives will change a student's thinking, value system and attitudes, and actions. In essence, how will these objectives change a student's behavior patterns?

The development of educational objectives is a matter of conscious choice on the part of the social studies teaching staff. The acceptance of the objectives reflects the educational philosophy of the faculty. One type of source generally used in the consideration of objectives is the information available about the students. For instance, what is their present level of development? What are their needs? What are their interests? An additional source for objective formulation is an analysis of the contemporary aspects of life confronting students. Furthermore, what are their career possibilities and what problems are they likely to encounter? Another significant source of suggestions for educational objectives is the particular social science disciplines which comprise the social studies curriculum. What is the nature of the subject matter being studied and what is its potential contribution for changing the behavior of secondary students?

In an ultimate sense, the objectives for the secondary social studies curriculum are examined in relation to how they contribute to the relationship between the student and society, at the present time and during his adult life.

Social Studies Objectives: The Affective Domain[15]

Affective objectives in social education emphasize a feeling, an emotion, or a degree of acceptance or rejection. Many of the traditional objectives of secondary social studies teachers lie in the affective domain. For instance, social studies teachers try to influence the attitudes of their students toward their course work. They want students to find satisfaction in responding creditably to homework assignments and classroom discussions. They want each student to examine his values, to organize them into a value system, and to develop a personal philosophy.

The first involves the choice of interests, attitudes, appreciations, values, and emotional biases to teach. The second problem involves classroom instruction itself. Much that social studies teachers do in the affective domain results from implicit rather than from explicit instruction. Teachers may instruct students to value the opinions of others by treating the statements made by their students with respect. Teachers may encourage students to find satisfaction in intellectual attainment by complimenting them on their written or oral presentations. Teachers can also attempt to attain affective objectives through explicit instruction, by examining the value systems of others or by teaching that a certain set of attitudes or values is to be preferred.

The third problem involves that of student evaluation. Obviously, cognitive objectives are quite easy to grade or evaluate through the traditional examination approach. The evaluation of affective objectives or the degree of attainment of attitudes and values is much more difficult to measure through structured examinations. Furthermore, the very nature of the social studies program which encourages relative thought and inquiry makes it difficult for teachers to grade students on individual interests, attitudes, value system, and moral development. Nevertheless, if affective objectives are to be established, continued efforts must be made to evaluate them.

Social Studies Objectives: The Cognitive Domain[16]

Most social studies courses in the secondary school are accompanied by curriculum guides and unit outlines which contain a list of objectives. Examination of these objectives reveals that the vast majority are cognitive in nature. Specifically, they are concerned with the acquisition of content knowledge and particular skills and abilities which complement the attainment of this knowledge.

There is little doubt that most secondary social studies instructors emphasize the teaching of knowledge objectives. Much of the teaching is absolute rather than interpretive in nature, with emphasis placed upon absolute facts such as names, dates, events, and so on. Furthermore, so much instructional time and energy is devoted to the teaching of knowledge and skill objectives that little if any attention is given to attitudes and values of the affective domain.

Cognitive objectives can be succinctly defined as:[17]

1. Knowledge objectives: the ability to recall or recognize ideas or phenomena that a student has experienced in the same form or in a similar form at an earlier time.
2. Abilities and skills: the ability to find appropriate information and techniques in a student's educational experience to help him make decisions and solve problems with which he will be confronted. Specific examples include the ability to think reflectively and in relative terms.

Among the major difficulties in the formulation of objectives for the secondary social studies are the complications which arise from defining behavioral objectives in terms of cognitive and affective.[18] This difficulty results from the disagreement among those teachers who place a great deal of significance and instructional priority upon subject matter content (knowledge and skill objectives) and those who emphasize the development of attitudes, values, and mental sets on the part of students. The essence of the argument involves the priority of content accumulation versus the priority of human behavior. In terms of the formulation of behavioral objectives, this philosophical polarization should not exist. Optimistically, there is increasing evidence that many experienced secondary social studies teachers are attempting to reduce this dichotomy through the utilization of innovative instructional techniques.

Closely related to the theory that social studies objectives — both knowledge and attitudinal objectives — should be capable of being measured in behavioral terms is the prerequisite that the objectives which are selected be consistent with research findings of educational psychology.[19] Obviously, some changes in behavior cannot be taught effectively. Some human characteristics are physiological or psychological in origin and cannot be significantly changed. Other behavioral patterns take so long to achieve that it is not feasible to attempt their accomplishment through the formal education program. Furthermore, it is argued by some that behavioral objectives, whether based upon knowledge or attitudinal patterns, should be relative and, therefore, not capable of measurement. This group bases its conclusion on what it considers to be the primary rationale of social studies education — that of instilling within students a mode of inquiry for the purpose of promoting interpretive and relative thought, which obviously results in relative rather than absolute behavioral objectives.

Supporters of behavioral objectives underscore that in the social studies classroom both the motivation and achievement of students is directly related to their knowing what to do and how well they perform. While these major advantages can be justified, there exist numerous other advantages for using behavioral objectives as a basis for curriculum planning in the social studies. Among the advantages stated for the use of behavioral objectives in classroom instruction, curriculum design, and teacher training are the following developed by a noted proponent of the behavioral approach:[20]

1. Behavioral objectives give both teachers and pupils a *clear sense of purpose.*

2. Behavioral objectives facilitate the fragmenting of content into *meaningful and manageable* pieces.
3. Behavioral objectives facilitate the *organizing of content* into hierarchies and therefore instructional sequence.
4. Behavioral objectives simplify *evaluative procedures*.
5. Behavioral objectives simplify the *training of teachers*.
6. Behavioral objectives *clarify the relevance* of particular pieces of instructional material.
7. Behavioral objectives open the educative process to *research and planning*.

RELEVANCE AND THE SECONDARY SOCIAL STUDIES

We are currently witnessing a period of history in which youth on a mass and international scale are rejecting and opposing many traditional educative processes. It is currently fashionable to reject past historical and social knowledge as irrelevant and to emphasize present behavioral patterns almost exclusively. However, much of what social studies educators currently emphasize is theoretically and practically irrelevant relevance! Indeed, there exists the widespread thesis with regard to relative content that no comprehension of any current social, economic, or political problem is possible if students fail to consider its genesis and development, that is, its history. Continuing, this school of thought holds that causation itself remains a mystery and, furthermore, solutions are impossible if causes are unknown.

Concerning the relevant nature of subject matter in the secondary social studies program, both experienced and pre-service teachers should be aware that subject matter or content emphasis is, philosophically speaking, a cyclic phenomenon, and relative within itself. For instance, since the inception of the existing secondary social studies curriculum during the second decade of the present century, both content emphasis and pedagogical technique twice have come full-circle, and are presently in the midst of a third cycle. Specifically, in terms of scope, the secondary social studies curriculum has alternated from national—to international—to national content stress and from a non-directive—directive—non-directive methodological rationale in less than half a century. In the opinion of many professional educators, it is vital that social studies teachers understand that what appears to be highly relevant content for today's secondary student won't necessarily constitute relevant subject matter for tomorrow's student or be synonymous with the social issues confronting these students as adults.

The human condition is in a constant and rapid state of change. The study of the past, the mastery of selected background knowledge, and the application of the results of such study in considering the present and future is crucially important for students and teachers living in an age of transition. Study of the past may alternatively be used to divert and confuse students in their thinking about the major social, economic, and political issues of their own historical period. A major challenge for the social studies teacher is to become involved in the process of content identification and selection of what is valid use and what is abuse of past events for the social education of today's students.

Relevancy and Curriculum Planning

Secondary students of the social sciences are becoming ever-increasingly critical of traditional educational practice. A widespread criticism among students is that the social studies curriculum lacks relevance in relation to the issues and events confronting mankind. In many instances, this situation is reminiscent of the type of criticism which launched the Progressive Era in American precollegiate education.

Obviously, students find it most easy to enumerate contradictions in the value systems and beliefs of their elders, and to conclude that all such discrepancies are succinct examples of hypocrisy. However, they are much less proficient in realizing their own inconsistencies, and they are quite convinced of their own sincerity. It has been suggested that the type of curricular relevance that education needs would encourage youth to reflect upon their most basic assumptions about the global societal condition, and how they propose to alter existing social institutions into something more preferable. However, in order to achieve this kind of relevance, social studies teachers must familiarize themselves with the thought patterns of students, for example, students' attitudes, values, beliefs, and interests. Four questions appear basic to future secondary social studies curriculum planning: (1) What kind of society now exists, and what are the predominant human trends within it? (2) What kind of a society is likely to develop by the end of the present century if current social trends continue? (3) On the basis of individual and societal values and ideals, what type of society is preferable for the United States? (4) If the predicted society appears to be different from the society that one prefers, what can the individual, alone or as a member of groups, contribute toward eliminating the discrepancy?

The continued search for a more relevant secondary social studies curriculum should have great appeal to those students who feel or believe that a drastic change in the contemporary social system is vital for the solution to the nation's social dilemmas. Its appeal lies in the fact that the search for relevance requires one to give conscientious consideration to the problem of the best approaches to achieve drastic curricular innovation which will facilitate significant changes at all levels of society.

CHAPTER 2

Methodological Change in Social Studies Instruction

MODERN INTUITIVE APPROACHES: INQUIRY AND REFLECTIVE STRATEGIES

A major recurring criticism of current social studies instruction is that the subject content is descriptive rather than interpretive, resulting in instructional techniques which encourage the accumulation of absolute facts rather than relative concepts. There exists nearly unanimous professional opinion that secondary social science teachers must develop more effective instructional strategies for introducing the skills of critical analysis to the consideration of subject matter topics for the purpose of improving students' ability to apply the inquiry method and reflect upon social issues in a relative rather than purely descriptive context. Throughout the history of American education, social studies teaching has been concerned almost exclusively with the promulgation of right or wrong answers and with the accumulation of descriptive facts, which are highly obsolescent, are not readily retained, and if retained, are retained only for a brief period.

Difficulties in Implementing Inquiry Techniques

Promoting the skills of critical inquiry and independent thinking in relative context has long been among the main behavioral objectives of social studies instruction. However, a variety of factors has militated against developing techniques of social studies instruction capable of motivating secondary students to become independent and creative thinkers.

One of the most valuable realizations that a beginning or experienced secondary social studies teacher can achieve is an awareness of the semantic haziness concerning the thinking process. In the professional literature, thinking is treated as a total process encompassing everything that goes on in the mind, from daydreaming to creating a concept about cybernetics. Even the most prominent educators, learning theorists, and educational psychologists have failed to distinguish between (1) the elements of thinking or the basic skills of which thinking is composed and (2) the strategies of thought, such as inquiry-oriented approaches or problem-solving, let alone effectively merging the elements and strategies of the thought process in the selection and presentation of subject matter. Styles of thinking such as convergent and divergent thinking, productive thinking, and critical thinking, are expounded simultaneously with fundamental processes such as concept formation, inferring, and generalizing.

This vagueness has resulted in enormous confusion, which every social studies teacher must attempt to interpret. The instructor must realize that there exists no systematic or structured formula for content selection, defining relevant or irrelevant content, or implementing the skills of critical inquiry. This situation, however, should not be interpreted negatively. Indeed, the relativity involved in the selection of subject matter and the opportunity to introduce innovative instructional procedures are thoroughly positive aspects of social studies teaching in that they encourage individualism and experimentation on the part of the teacher.

There is widespread agreement that the ultimate objectives of social studies instruction are threefold: (1) to instill within students the skills and abilities vital to the decision-making process, (2) to motivate a desire for continued learning throughout the student's lifetime, and (3) to prepare students to function productively in a complex and ever-changing national and international society. How to accomplish these objectives most effectively represents both the challenge and reward of social studies teaching.

The Social Studies Methods Course

There is little doubt that most secondary social science teachers could be better equipped to undertake their responsibilities in terms of both subject matter preparation and cognizance of instructional techniques. Regarding the latter, criticism of the social studies methods course continues to be nearly universal among pre-service and in-service teachers. It would seem, however, that the answer is not to delete the methods course but to improve it. Traditionally, the coverage in methods courses has been limited literally to teaching "methods" while the academic offerings in the social sciences have and will continue to deal entirely with "content." This polarization of pedagogical sterility within subject matter courses and academic sterility within methods courses has resulted in a most apparent void in the professional preparation of secondary social studies teachers. Obviously, teacher education programs cannot consist of a series of three or four "special methods" courses, for example, a methods course in history offered by a historian, or a methods course in civics and government taught by a political scientist. However, it would appear feasible that the professional training of secondary social studies teachers in the social sciences could be strengthened substantially by designing one basic methods course comprising the social science disciplines and utilizing a "team teaching" approach which would involve several instructors with competency both in the specific academic areas and in modern instructional strategies as well as practical classroom experience in the processes of content translation at the secondary level. The development of a "substantive methods" course, in which content and methodology are complementary and, thus, synonymous, remains one of the foremost tasks confronting social scientists and social studies teachers.

Implementing Inquiry and Reflective Techniques

The effective utilization of the inquiry method in social education is based upon the formulation of hypotheses or assumptions concerning aspects of the human condition. Through examining and questioning the assumptions, students may develop and refine their skills of critical analysis. Successful development of these skills and their continued application to the consideration of vital contemporary issues will improve students' abilities to apply the inquiry method and reflect upon social issues in a relative rather than purely descriptive context.

At the conclusion of each major topic or theme being studied in the social studies class, the teacher should design assumptions for student inquiry. For classroom purposes, each theme and the accompanying assumptions might be reproduced and presented to the entire class, which should motivate spontaneous and unstructured discussion and debate. A more effective instructional technique, however, would be to divide the social studies class into the appropriate number of subgroups and assign each group one major theme and the suggested assumptions. Individual group members would then be responsible for stating hypotheses, undertaking independent

research, formulating generalizations, and either accepting or rejecting one or two assumptions, depending on the number of students in
each group, on the basis of collected data. The group leaders might
then summarize and present the research findings and conclusions of
each group to the remainder of the class. A more structural approach
would be for the individual group members to be responsible for
stating the assumptions and reporting the results of their research and
their tentative conclusions. With individual presentation of research
techniques, evidence, and conclusions, a higher level of motivation
and critical inquiry might be attained for both the particular student
and the class; this could be the result of the positive and negative
criticism which should arise from the opportunity to justify research
procedures, validity of evidence, and resultant conclusions. Furthermore, group data collecting and reporting can provide numerous opportunities to meet the different needs of individual students as well
as to teach the complex skills required for working effectively with
others.

SIMULATION AND GAMING TECHNIQUES

From the methodological point of view, one of the most pub-
licized instructional techniques in the history of American social
studies instruction is the strategy referred to as simulation gaming.
By definition, a simulation game is quite similar to socio-drama or
role-playing, which have been used for sometime in both social
studies classrooms and in the professional education of social studies
teachers. Simulation allows for students to actively participate in
"real situations" of a domestic or international nature by assuming
the roles of individuals or nations.

Examples of Simulation Games

For instance, in a simulated domestic or national crisis students
may play the roles of President, congressional and Cabinet leaders,
and other national officials and determine what decisions they would
make in terms of crisis and its threat to the nation. A second example
of a domestic issue which might be simulated for active student participation would be a strike by organized labor. In this simulation,
individual students would play the roles of particular labor leaders
and union officials, representatives from management, and, if the
labor-management dispute could not be settled through collective

bargaining, individual students would have to assume the roles of government mediators in an attempt to arbitrate or settle the strike. Examples of simulations of an international nature would be a mock United Nations game in which students would assume the role of representatives and their advisers in General Assembly meetings or meetings of the Security Council. One of the most common simulations in international relations involves the actual threat of war between two or more nations. In this game, the class might be divided on the basis of the number of nations involved in the international dispute, with individual students representing government and military leaders of the various nations. The main theme of the simulation would involve the decisions, concessions, and strategic considerations the representatives of each nation would make, on the basis of their national interests and security, to prevent war or to sustain a war effort if an international conflict developed. One of the most significant attributes of this approach as a classroom technique is the number of different topics and events which may be simulated.

Motivation and the Decision-Making Process

From the methodological and behavioristic standpoints, simulations which are systematically directed by the classroom teacher possess two positive characteristics. First, they are highly motivational if some structure is provided. Second, students become actively involved in the decision-making process by simulating the actual responsibilities and reactions of the individuals in a domestic or international issue. Students have the direct opportunity to experience either the positive or negative consequences of specific decisions.

Two fundamental criticisms of secondary social studies instruction is that it is extremely difficult to provide for student motivation and, second, little instructional emphasis is placed upon preparing students to make political, economic, social, and personal decisions as adolescents or adults. The evidence provided by current research of simulation techniques indicates that well defined and organized simulations make significant contributions to the attainment of both objectives.

Organizing Simulation Games

In addition to the wide range of simulation games available from commercial publishers,[1] teachers as well as students may design simulations to apply to nearly any national or international issue. When developing an instructional strategy based upon simulation, social studies teachers should observe the following principles:

1. The international or domestic issue selected for a simulation game should be of significant interest or relevance to the entire class.
2. Provide leadership and direction in structuring a simulation that will achieve the desired behavioral objectives.
3. At the conclusion of the simulation, provide an opportunity for students to discuss its strengths and weaknesses.

With proper guidance, simulation games may be dynamic instructional techniques in terms of developing student behavior, achieving fundamental educational objectives, and providing a base for teacher innovation and creativity.

INTERDISCIPLINARY APPROACHES IN SECONDARY EDUCATION

The social sciences lack clear-cut boundaries delimiting one subject matter area from another. Indeed, both sociology and anthropology are sometimes considered as extraneous sciences because they have undertaken the study of subject matter that would appear to be within the academic boundaries of other disciplines but not emphasized by them. Most of the pioneering research on political socialization, for instance, was done by sociologists rather than political scientists.[2] Similarly, many believe that sociology and cultural anthropology are nearly alike in many respects. Furthermore, political scientists and economists both examine the relationships that exist between government and various economic sectors, and political science courses dealing with comparative political systems and international relations include much material of a geographic, historical, and economic nature. Similarly, geographers also draw upon history, cultural anthropology, economics, and sociology to describe the unique characteristics of various global regions.[3]

There are some who believe that the social sciences may eventually be incorporated into one overall study of human behavior. In higher education, however, there have been few successful attempts to develop integrated or interdisciplinary approaches in the social sciences. Nevertheless, the social sciences have a great deal in common, particularly in their overlap of subject matter, and complement one another both directly and indirectly.

Integrating the Social Sciences in the Secondary Curriculum

Interdisciplinary approaches in the precollegiate social studies curriculum have proved much more successful than in higher education, due, primarily, to necessity. Traditionally, the secondary social studies curriculum has reflected the collegiate organization of the social sciences with regard to several basic content areas. For instance, courses in United States history, world history, and geography are the most clear-cut examples of the transfer downward from higher education to secondary education. On the other hand, while the collegiate social science curriculum has expanded and proliferated separate disciplines, the secondary curriculum has witnessed an integrative approach to such content areas as economics, government, sociology, and social psychology into one basic course commonly titled "Problems of Democracy" and "Civics."[4] Similarly, newer courses referred to as "world cultures" or "area studies" commonly emphasize a close integration of Western and non-Western history and geography.

The Rationale for Interdisciplinary Curriculum Planning

The major argument advanced for an integrated social science program involves the hypothesis that societies, culture, and civilizations are simple entities. Each social institution, and each social process which comprises it, contributes to the development of the whole entity and is conditioned by it. Therefore, this thesis holds that subject matter which contributes to the understanding of any cultural or social topic must be related to the whole, before an understanding of the particular human or cultural topic can be understood. In essence, it is widely held by influential educators that an integrative approach to the subject matter disciplines promotes a more comprehensive curriculum.[5] Furthermore, the most expedient manner in which to introduce materials from the many and newer social sciences into the already overburdened secondary social studies program is to introduce data and concepts from the academic social sciences into existing social studies courses. As noted above, anthropology, economics, social psychology, and sociology have become components of the secondary curriculum primarily through this integral approach.

It must be emphasized that social studies teachers and professional educators who support integrated curriculum planning are not in any way negating either the distinct organization framework of the social sciences in higher education or the research efforts of scholars in the individual disciplines. However, in terms of both the limited time factor in the secondary curriculum and the view that if the research data from the separate social science disciplines are to be used to achieve the objectives of general education rather than specialized scholarship, secondary social studies courses must reflect the integration and innovation of new knowledge and theories discovered by academic social scientists.

Combining information and data from two or more social science disciplines into one secondary social studies course has definite academic advantages, in the view of many educators. First, the integration of materials from different disciplines within a particular social studies subject motivates students to achieve a better comprehension of the subject matter interrelationships which exist among the social science disciplines. Second, such a procedure reinforces the flexibility of curriculum planning. For instance, particular materials and topics can be implemented with greater convenience in several social studies subject areas.[6] In addition, when considering current affairs the discussion will, in most instances, be of an interdisciplinary nature. Thus, students must develop the ability to visualize the various academic components of a current topic and discuss it on an integrated basis.

Likewise, the integration of subject matter into secondary social studies courses possesses certain disadvantages. Specifically, it must be considered negative if college-bound secondary students fail to come into contact with at least some systematically organized social science disciplines in their secondary education. Furthermore, the availability and suitability of multi-disciplinary texts, references, and other instructional materials confronts an integrated curriculum with a definite problem. An additional problem is one of finding teachers with adequate preparation in several of the social sciences and with acceptable levels of competency in various instructional techniques.[7]

In conclusion, it is practical to recognize that each of the social science disciplines cannot be given individual attention as a separate course offering in the secondary social studies curriculum. Avid supporters of integrated courses place a priority upon what topics and issues should be taught rather than which of the specific subject fields. As a result, the teachers' primary responsibility in an integrated social studies curriculum is one of content selection from the various social science disciplines.

Interdisciplinary Area-Studies Programs

Educators who favor integrated social studies courses at the secondary level point to the relatively new and, perhaps, the most successful, interdisciplinary approach involving the social sciences in higher education—the various area-study programs. One of the most significant developments in American higher education since World War II has been the rapid development of global area studies—a study of specific world regions which utilizes the integration of the various disciplines such as geography, history, economics, and political science, and sociology.[8] In most instances, the area under consideration includes one large political entity such as the Soviet Union, the People's Republic of China, the United States, or a regional combination of smaller nations such as the Near East, Subsaharan Africa, south Asia, or Latin America. Most significant, however, is that the particular areas or regions are studied from the points of view representing several academic disciplines. As a result, a better understanding of the interrrelationships existing among the various disciplines is achieved through the application of several content fields to the consideration of one political unit. Additionally, area-studies programs in higher education tend to moderate or even break down the traditional academic boundaries which continue to exist among the disciplines. In relation to the secondary curriculum, the significance of the multi-disciplinary area-study approach in collegiate education lies in the hope that scholars are recognizing the necessity for broadening their disciplinary scope when studying particular issues and topics and that this attitude will transfer to the secondary curriculum, thus reinforcing integrated approaches in the social studies. Furthermore, the offering of area-study programs in the secondary social studies is becoming more widespread, largely as a result of interdisciplinary studies in colleges and universities. The hopeful expectation is that the whole will be greater than the sum of the parts, and that a broader and more thorough comprehension will result from multi-disciplinary area-studies than can be gained by studying other culture regions through only one discipline or methodological point of view.[9]

CHAPTER 3

Teaching Contemporary Domestic Issues: Interdisciplinary Themes

In recent years, a major thrust in secondary social studies education has been to place much more emphasis upon the consideration of both contemporary domestic issues and temporary international issues utilizing interdisciplinary techniques, regardless of the particular course or subject in which the specific topic might be studied. This curricular trend has been motivated largely by the concern expressed by both students and faculty members that serious attempts should be made to make the secondary social studies curriculum more relevant in order to meet the needs of American youth in their attempt to live, positively function, and compete in their contemporary national and global societies, which are becoming ever-increasingly complex. Significantly, the best available evidence supports the assumption that the teaching of interdisciplinary topics or issues of a contemporary nature will continue to gain prominence as a vital component of the social studies program and, perhaps, may emerge as the most significant innovation in the secondary social studies curriculum of the second half of the twentieth century.

DEFINING CONTEMPORARY ISSUES

A distinction must be made at this point in the discussion between a contemporary issue or affair and a current event. Unlike current events, a contemporary issue is a topic in which continuing developments should take place and, second, is an issue which should possess significant social, political, or economic relevance in terms of the immediate and future impact on the lives of today's secondary students. A contemporary affair, therefore, will involve those central issues which have a greater degree of permanence and a more

34

significant effect upon the domestic and international scene. As noted above, particular current events may emerge into current affairs of lasting significance, but the great majority of current news items should be limited to passing rather than systematic classroom attention, especially at the secondary level.

RACIAL-CULTURAL INTEGRATION AND MINORITY-GROUP RELATIONS

As is the case in all advanced nations, governmental policy at the community, state, and national levels must continually promote a policy of racial and minority-group integration. Such a social policy is vital to the achievement of civil rights and, ultimately, to national security, since no nation can afford to risk substantial segments of its population—due to minority traits or traditions—to be outside the economic, political, and cultural mainstream of society. In the interest of national viability, therefore, every attempt must be made to strive toward the achievement of this goal.

Throughout the entire educational system, elementary through higher education, the social science curriculum has the primary responsibility, in relation to all other curricular areas, for developing the instructional strategies that will eventually achieve the objective of improving minority-group relations and instilling within American youth the necessary cross-cultural attitudes and values to achieve an integrated society.

The Social Studies Curriculum in Urban Areas

The challenge confronting the secondary social studies teacher in promoting the values and ideals of social equality is, obviously, most prominent in the metropolitan school systems. Furthermore, all of the evidence indicates that applying the standard test of quality—specifically, the impact that traditional social studies instruction has had upon instilling more positive attitudes toward minority groups and disadvantaged youths—has largely failed in this objective. As a result, urban education is paying a heavy price for its apparent shortcomings, including an increasing lack of confidence in public education.[1]

The city's poor—usually blacks, Mexican-American, and/or other minorities—have little choice but the public schools for their children's education. In the nation's major urban areas, black populations are increasingly becoming majorities, if not in total city population, then certainly in city school population. For instance, in the District of Columbia more than 93 percent of the school population is black. In New York, Philadelphia, and Chicago, the proportion is well over 50 percent.[2] Indeed, in a society which will become nearly 80 percent urban (nearly 80 percent of the American people will reside in Standard Statistical Metropolitan Areas defined as cities of 50,000 or more, by the end of the present decade)[3] when we speak of urban education we are, in reality, speaking of American education.

In the urban school, the secondary social studies curriculum, if it is to meet the goals of integration, must be broadened to restore a quality that has been sidetracked during the contemporary emphasis on traditional academic achievement. Secondary social studies teachers must achieve the recognition that instilling proper attitudes and promoting an awareness among students of cultural diversity and differences are assets in a democratic society. Furthermore, encouraging such an attitude is just as significant an instructional goal and will have, perhaps, a more positive effect on student growth and development as the teaching of traditional academic skills.

Cultural Integration, Assimulation, and Social Studies Instruction

In the urban social studies curriculum, the terminology "education for life adjustment" must achieve practical significance and emphasis if the objective of racial integration is to be achieved. The label "life adjustment education" was officially applied to a new program of curriculum innovation and improvement in the social studies at the conclusion of World War II.[4] Immediately, however, this new curricular proposal was criticized severely by the advocates of the traditional liberal arts approach to the secondary social studies program. However, if the secondary social sciences are to fulfill their objective of promoting improved societal relations in urban schools, a definite compromise must be achieved between supporters of one concept of life adjustment education, for example, a social studies curriculum that places a priority upon meeting the problems confronting American youths in their contemporary society, and the traditionalists who support a secondary curriculum based upon systematically organized academic courses. Such a compromise, however, may be achieved successfully if social studies teachers and educators representing both points of view can agree that emphasizing instructional materials in contemporary, social, political, and economic issues (in this instance, minority-group relations and racial integration) can be readily integrated into existing and traditionally oriented social studies courses.

Cultural-Racial Assimilation as a Goal of Social Education

Throughout the remainder of the twentieth century the secondary social studies will make an outstanding contribution to the American human condition if it can achieve substantial progress toward the achievement of cultural assimilation among the various segments of the nation's population. It would seem that to emphasize integration among the races in a locational sense only will fall far short of achieving the ultimate goal of socializing the various demographic elements comprising American society. Indeed, minority-group peoples must be accepted in a psychological sense by the vast majority of the white population before the terms civil rights and integration will have any valid significance. Thus, the social studies program must emphasize assimilation between the minority groups and the white majority. Specifically, this implies that social studies instructors must instill positive values, ideals, and respect and strive to promote the "appropriate mental set" among students representing all racial groups. Only when acceptance of others is achieved in psychological terms can racial prejudice be eliminated and true integration (assimilation) be achieved.

TEACHING CONTROVERSIAL SOCIETAL ISSUES

It is extremely difficult to teach objectively about values and ideals in a highly complex urbanized society, particularly one which is undergoing rapid technological and sociological change. When discussing controversial issues, the secondary social studies teacher is confronted with three basic problems. First, regardless of continued efforts to motivate critical inquiry, most students want positive answers to societal issues and problems of a controversial nature. Too often they appear to demand some absolute measure for determining if a particular social, economic, or political issue is right or wrong or if supporting or rejecting a particular position concerning the human condition is good or bad. With regard to most issues of a controversial nature, there are no final right or wrong answers. Second, a recurring criticism of contemporary social studies instruction when teaching about controversial issues is that the content of the discussion is descriptive rather than interpretive, resulting in instructional techniques which encourage the accumulation of absolute facts, often highly biased in nature, rather than relative concepts. Third, the individual social studies teacher is faced with the socioeconomic values and mores which have traditionally existed in the particular urban school district or community. Obviously, there is a great deal of pressure, fear, and the threat of potential or actual loss of employment resulting from questioning or challenging particular values and social mores. These problems, however, are inherent in social studies teaching, unlike secondary mathematics, foreign language, the natural and physical sciences, and so on. For this reason, one of the primary responsibilities of the secondary social studies teacher is to promote objective classroom discussions of controversial issues. Additionally, students will have a higher degree of respect for the teacher who gives the various views of an issue, including his own, if such opinions are supported by some kind of valid evidence. Such an approach will do much more to encourage critical inquiry on the part of students than either ignoring areas of controversy, simply reinforcing community values, or giving opinionated and emotional solutions.

Religious Instruction in Secondary Social Studies

Religion is taught in the secondary social studies whether there is an overt systematic attempt to do so or not. The significant question confronting curriculum planners in the social studies is not whether religion should be an integral part of public education but, rather, how and to what extent religion should be taught.[5] The American Association of School Administrators made this point clearly when they said: "A curriculum which ignored religion would itself have serious religious implications. It would seem to proclaim that religion has not been as real in men's lives as health or politics or economics. By omission it would appear to deny that religion has been and is important in man's history — a denial of the obvious."[6]

The secondary social studies curriculum will inevitably give attention to religion, since it has been forced to include most of the basic issues confronting mankind. Furthermore, the school should give attention to religion because of the continually greater influence the formal educational program exerts upon the student. In essence, the supporters of the consideration of religious topics within the social studies curriculum emphasize that such study is requisite to a good general education. The U.S. Supreme Court, when limiting the practice of religion in public educational systems, strongly suggested in its interpretation of the issue that education is not complete without the study of religion.[7]

There appears to be widespread consensus among the best intellectual minds both without as well as within the organized religious establishment that the secondary social science curriculum should teach no particular religion or religious thought but will provide an opportunity to study many religions.[8] Certainly not all religions will be considered to the same degree. Student motivation, together with curriculum guidelines and available time, will, to a significant degree, determine the amount of attention devoted to various religious philosophies. A major point to be emphasized is that the rationale for religious instruction will not be to convince the student to believe in one particular religion or another, rather, to expose the student to various religious viewpoints in global perspective. To quote the recent interpretation of the U.S. Supreme Court once again, "One's education is not complete without a study of comparative religion or the history of religion and its relationship to the advancement of civilization."[9]

Many top-flight secondary school systems are currently integrating units on religion within existing social studies courses, most commonly in grades nine through twelve. A sampling of the types of religious philosophies considered reveals such units as "Primitive Religions," "Religions of the Far East," "Middle Eastern Religions," "Introduction to World Religions," and "Religions of the Western World."[10] From an examination of these instructional units it is obvious that the public educational systems represented in no way violate the principle of separation of church and state. Indeed, separation of church and state applies to the control of one over the other. The separation is absolute in the area of control: the state must not control the church nor the church the state. Obviously, then, when a public school curriculum gives consideration to a particular religion or several religions in the context of subject matter content there is contact between church and state but there exists no violation of the principle of separation.

Sex Education in the Social Studies Program

One of the most controversial and bitterly contested domestic issues to confront the secondary schools since the inception of public education in the United States involves the problem of whether or not to offer systematic structured instruction in sex education. Furthermore, the particular nature of this debate will probably continue for the foreseeable future. Although the social studies is not the only curricular field to be affected by this issue, it will probably be just as directly responsible for instruction in this area as any other secondary program.

The proponents of a systematic instructional program of sex education base their case upon a synthesis of the following arguments: Sex education in public education is as vital to the education of the nation's youth as education in the areas of English, the traditional social sciences and humanities, the biological and physical sciences, and mathematics.[11] The opponents of sex education base their opposition on the assumption that such instruction will result in a breakdown of the Judeo-Christian or Puritanical ethic of morality among adolescents and will encourage more premarital sexual experimentation, a higher venereal disease rate, more illegitimate children, more sexual perversion, and so on, than currently exists.

The extreme controversial nature of the issue emerges when both the proponents and opponents become involved in the debate over such topics as what constitutes morality, perversion, pornography, as well as the diverse psychological theories concerning controlled versus complete sexual freedom — in essence, the lack of universally accepted values or attitudes of what constitutes psychologically and physiologically good or bad sexual behavior, to say nothing of the relativity involved in the issue of what is right and what is wrong in terms of sexual conduct. This latter situation is underscored by the fact that psychological and psychiatric experts are divided on nearly every issue concerning human sexual behavior.

The social studies teacher who is or may be responsible for sex education instruction should be aware of several major considerations. First, that this subject is probably the most emotional of all the contemporary controversial issues in public education. Second, that sex education materials contain an extremely wide range of relativity and that descriptive, absolute, and final answers will be impossible to structure. Third, the accepted societal attitudes toward sexual behavior will, in many instances, vary considerably in different areas of the nation, with the greatest variance existing between rural communities and larger urban areas. Similarly, sexual mores will vary between where the students are presently attending school and where many of them will move to attend college and spend their adult lives. Finally, the teacher must attempt to be as objective as possible, using the best evidence and instructional materials he can acquire and be prepared to defend his position and methods before the administrative officers of the school system, the parents, various civic and religious groups in the community, and lay representatives of the general public.

In conclusion, it is the opinion of this writer that the experienced or prospective teacher should give serious thought to the following assumption regarding sex education in the schools: It would appear that both the opponents and proponents of sex education have the same ultimate goal in mind regarding sex education—that of attempting to preserve the basic elements of human sexual behavior as interpreted by the Judeo-Christian ethic and social tradition. The objective is the same, only the method of how best to achieve this goal is different.

Drug Abuse Education

Although this topic is not considered to be strictly within the academic limits of the secondary social studies, there is little doubt that it probably will receive more attention in such classes than in any other major curricular area. Similar to promoting discussions involving other controversial topics, the social studies instructor must develop the dialogue around the relative aspects of the drug abuse situation in the United States. He should not introduce scare tactics nor should he attempt to expound absolute negative or positive answers concerning the use of drugs.

One approach for promoting an objective discussion of this topic in social studies classes is to compare the use of drugs to the use and abuse of alcohol in American society. Such a discussion will involve three major themes for student consideration. First, to what extent does peer or social pressure initiate the use of drugs among elementary and secondary students? Second, since the problem of drug abuse appears to be a symptom, what appears to be the basic causes which produce such symptoms? Third, will the use of soft drugs eventually be treated legally in the same respect as the use of alcohol? By developing the classroom instruction around these three themes, the social studies teacher is involving students in those areas of human concern in which he has some level of competence, namely, in the behavior patterns of individuals. The teacher should not become involved in the physiological and psychological aspects of drug usage. When these dimensions of the drug situation are to be considered, it is vital that individuals competent in these fields be invited as guest lecturers or consultants.

URBANIZATION AND POST-TECHNOLOGICAL SOCIETY

There are now more than 207 million Americans. If present growth patterns continue, the United States will reach a population of more than 300 million by the year 2000 and its major metropolitan areas will absorb most of the increase. This population growth and the massive urban explosion that accompanies it have created problems of great magnitude for American cities. This expanding populace must be educated, housed, employed, and transported. Their health, recreational, and cultural needs must also be met.[12]

Currently approximately 72 percent of the American people reside in urban areas. Demographic projections[13] indicate that during the decade of the seventies this urban proportion will increase by more than 60 million people, an increase demanding some 20 cities the size of Los Angeles. Similar projections indicate that by the year 2000, 85 percent of the American population of 300 million will be urban.[14] Furthermore, it must be remembered that the United States has become an urban society with the complex social and psychological problems that such a phenomenon creates.

Changing Social Patterns

A major impact of a rapidly changing social and technological environment has been to drastically alter the cultural composition of the nation's urban areas. Less than 50 years ago, the majority of America's racial minority groups lived in the rural area; presently more than 70 percent (predominantly blacks) live in cities. In the District of Columbia, for example, currently more than 93 percent of the school population is black. In New York, Philadelphia, and Chicago, the figures are well over 50 percent. Thus, in a society in which nearly 80 percent of the populace will be living in cities by 1980, a discussion of urban education equals a discussion of American education.[15]

Three primary events influenced this radical alteration in the traditional urban social pattern. First, technological developments — particularly the automobile — opened vast areas around cities to settlement. Second, federal housing legislation created the Federal Housing Administration and enabled millions of Americans to obtain the credit necessary for home ownership. Third, the significance of class and ethnic difference became obvious as a result of the internal migration to the inner cities of millions of blacks and other minority groups. The result of these racial relocations in the social pattern of the urban area was to remove the basis of the white middle-class majority, leaving only a very small minority of wealth and affluence and a lower-class (largely non-white) majority.[16] While these changes were taking place, changes were also taking place in the structure and quality of education in the central cities which have created numerous problems for metropolitan school systems.

Social Studies and the Urban Environment

Secondary social studies teachers are responsible for instilling attitudes in adolescents that can affect the course of American history. The nation currently is confronted with great unrest. Change is cutting across outmoded traditions and values, and progress is being made toward bridging and narrowing the gap between the races. Youths are in the vanguard of this change, and their idealism is a priceless human resource for furthering this nation's progress. No profession is more challenging nor more rewarding than teaching young people to view domestic problems clearly and objectively, and then to achieve solutions.

Urban problems are among the most crucial domestic issues confronting the social studies teachers. The social studies concept of human interdependence must be made more relevant to modern urban problems. For instance, the migration of middle-class white residents to suburbia and the demand of black separatists for a new kind of segregated life in the United States is evidence of the lack of understanding that the two elements of the major metropolitan area (the urban and suburban) are dependent upon each other and, for educational purposes, must be considered an integral unit.[17]

Students must not only achieve an awareness of metropolitan interdependence in the United States. They must view this phenomenon in relation to the world which is continually becoming much more socially, culturally, and economically interdependent. The global populations are now, more than ever, dependent on each other for peace. The problems of overpopulation, pollution, and divisiveness that exist between urban and suburban population are global phenomena.[18]

Since urban students represent a wide heterogeneous group, social studies teachers must develop their own concepts of democratic relationships, which would include understanding of the genetics of human races, the concepts of group similarities and group differences, and a valid illustration of stereotypes, discrimination, and prejudice.[19]

It is vital that the social studies in urban school systems encourage the discussion of relevant controversial issues. Introducing a new social studies program in urban and suburban secondary schools will not contribute much to promote inquiry among students concerning their relationship to their physical and cultural environment. Students learn best by relating to relevant concrete issues. What could be more concrete than understanding the problems that students in urban areas live, that they view about their home environment on television, that they hear discussed in their homes and at school among their classmates.[20]

Students are bombarded through the mass media by racial conflicts, group dissent, and other happenings of a similar nature but often teachers are hesitant to discuss these news events in their classrooms. Usually, it is in the central or inner city where such events are most common; therefore, a study of the human condition and the characteristics of disadvantaged youth in the inner city would be incomplete without discussing these events. Social studies teachers must attempt to stimulate youth to view firsthand the results of crowding many ethnic groups into a ghetto, the disparity in socioeconomic characteristics of the suburbanite and the ghetto resident, and the high density of Negroes and other racial minorities in the inner city, as these phenomena result in the societal pressures that explode into racial conflict.[21]

Historical Significance of Urbanism

If the instructional techniques in urban studies in the metropolitan area have to be varied, then the instructional materials employed in these studies must be varied also. Obviously, there is an agglomeration of materials on urban living, highly nebulous in description and which is probably meaningless to students living in the inner city.[22] Indeed, if teaching about urban life is to have genuine significance, it should be based upon the obvious and the substantial. What constitutes valid learning experiences for these students in social studies classes results from a consideration of the past as they have contributed to present-day life in the urban area.

Many of the issues that educators now refer to as "urban problems" or the "urban crisis" have characterized the American city for at least a century and in many instances longer. A classroom atmosphere in which students are directed to inquire into the past causes of present situations are much better equipped to comprehend the city as it exists today, and what possible alternative solutions are needed to improve the human condition in urban areas.

To instruct students about the inner city in which they reside or to describe the living conditions existing in the inner city to suburban, small town, or rural students, by emphasizing the state of physical and human decadence and environmental deterioration, accomplishes little to promote valid understanding among any of the student groups described above. A much more positive approach would be to point out the background of the forces that have contributed to the negative urban condition, namely, urban decay, racial conflict, substandard housing, drug abuse, alcoholism, crime, and so on.

Urban areas develop only by attracting people from the country-side, whether from rural America, Ireland, or Japan. Thus, one of the significant historic functions of cities the world over has been to transform rural man into urban man. In its Model Cities application, for example, Newark, New Jersey, described itself as having served over the decades as "a basic training camp for the poor."[23] Most large American cities have performed the same function throughout their history, particularly in an effort to develop a labor force to increase economic development.

Economic growth, however, resulted in more factories and more crowded cities. Appalled by the negative consequences of urban growth as they affected the human condition, educators hoped that greater economic opportunity would improve the deteriorating social condition and provide cohesive force lacking in the families and neighborhoods of the laboring class. One might assume that the urban school of the mid- and late nineteenth century was not committed to developing the potential of students as individuals but, rather, with the development of a human resource for the rapidly expanding economic system.[24] Educators, however, soon discovered that environmental decay, human deterioration, poverty, and crime developed more rapidly than the school population.

One approach to explaining the current plight of the nation's urban areas could be an examination of economic growth and development under late nineteenth- and early twentieth-century definitions of capitalism which placed priority upon machines over men. A second theme which social studies teachers could examine would be that of contemporary political procedures. During the last 20 years there has been a definite political shift in the balance of political power in metropolitan areas which has resulted in the people of the inner city having much less political influence. Obviously, significant decisions concerning financial appropriations for education, housing, and a plethora of other urban improvements have been seriously lacking, since many of the decisions affecting the urban condition have been influenced by small, influential suburban groups rather than on the basis of what would be beneficial to the residents of the inner city. Since the solution of suburban problems continues to receive priority, many central city problems continue unabated—the increasing crime rate being a case in point.

A third technique which could be introduced on a historical or chronological basis could be the sociological reality of the concept of "upward mobility"[25] in a social sense. This concept has had different implications for different racial groups of the inner city, depending upon skin color. Students need to achieve the awareness that white immigrants and minority groups have traditionally found it much easier to "climb the ladder" to economic, social, and political influence than dark-skinned people. Thus, generations of west European immigrants have benefited from their urban residence and employment while black and other non-European immigrants have been segregated in the confines of the ghetto.

The use of the historical method to illustrate some of the causal factors existing in today's inner city is a valid approach as long as the evidence presented is objective as possible. Social studies teachers are obviously aware of the ease with which events of the past can be slanted to the benefit of one racial or ethnic group at the expense of others. Such historical misinterpretations that have and continue to exist in social studies materials have resulted in the widespread clamor for such courses as "Black History" and "Black Studies" in the secondary social studies curriculum. However, the major problem with "Black Studies" courses is how to teach these courses in a manner which will not result in the kind of white nationalism, black nationalism, or racial ethnocentrism that currently exists in the nation. Positively, the ultimate objective of such courses is to examine the means and processes by which racial minorities can enter the mainstream of American economic and social life. Conversely, "Black Studies" programs which are open only to black students or white students will probably do more to reinforce than alleviate racial prejudice.[26]

Technology and the Human Condition

A fundamental result of urbanism and economic growth in economically advanced nations such as the United States is the continued development of scientific and technological achievements. As a result, the ability to function, make a living, be transported from one place to another, raise a family, and so on, becomes much more complex.

The stresses and strains pressuring the human organism increase rather than decrease in direct correlation with technological advancement. Furthermore, whatever the chosen job or profession, the level of competition continues to increase as the nation continues its unceasing trend of urbanization. A universal principle is that the city serves as a source of gravity for the most talented in every walk of life. In most instances, it is only in the city where the educated can fully realize their potential and be awarded for it in a material sense. Hence, the competition will continue to increase, resulting in increased complexities and pressures on the individual.

It is a primary responsibility of the secondary social studies teacher to consider these urban complexities in detail with students. This responsibility applies to teachers in rural communities, small towns, and medium-sized cities, as well as in major metropolitan areas. There is little doubt that the majority of today's secondary students will spend their adult lives in the city. The trend toward urbanization appears irreversible. For this reason, it is vital for the student's economic success, physiological health, and family and group relationships that he is made aware of the many and varied urban complexities and how to live a profitable and productive life in the urban environment.

In conclusion, the manner in which urban studies are presented in the classroom setting is highly significant if the ultimate educational objectives are to be achieved. A priority must be placed upon individual attention, so that students' values, attitudes, and abilities will be directed in positive directions to produce conscientious and responsible citizens. To achieve such results demands innovative, creative, open-minded instructors who can develop a classroom atmosphere conducive to the pursuance of improving the urban human condition.

SOCIAL EDUCATION FOR DISADVANTAGED YOUTH

The Great Depression of the 1930s, World War II, and the population boom that followed brought about a drastic change in the populations of the cities and, obviously, in the educational systems that served them.[27] As the suburbs mushroomed with the flight of the white middle class from the central cities, political and financial support for city schools declined. In the inner-city schools, the children of the poor, the new migrants, and those whose race or ethnic backgrounds prevented them from joining the outflow remained.

As a result of the urban population redistribution, urban schools became largely segregated on the basis of income, race, and ethnic origin. Most large city systems have cores of inner-city schools, located in depressed areas and surrounded by schools serving more affluent students. Indeed, the discrepancies in the educational attainment levels in schools of different social class characteristics are obvious. Inundated in poverty, unemployment, inadequate housing, unstable family life, lack of political influence, and community devisiveness, inner-city schools find pupils unresponsive to curricula which seem irrelevant and inappropriate. All of this has been known for decades, but very little action was taken to alleviate it. However, during the 1960s, the war on poverty and the civil rights movement combined to provide the impetus for action in the schools.

Programs for Disadvantaged Youth

During the late 1950s several significant developments began to be implemented for inner-city schools. As a result such terms as the inner-city child, socially disadvantaged, and culturally deprived began to appear.

It was the Elementary and Secondary Education Act of 1965 (ESEA) that provided the greatest impetus for programs in the schools with disadvantaged youth. In Title I of ESEA, the federal government acknowledged "the special educational needs of children of low-income families and the impact that concentrations of low-income families have on the ability of local educational agencies to support adequate educational programs."

Within a short time the following patterns for improving educational opportunity for disadvantaged youths began to emerge:

1. Pre-school and early childhood programs aimed at compensating for early experiential deficits, especially those of language and cognitive development.
2. Reassessment and development of curriculum content to facilitate acculturation in an urbanized, technological society.
3. Remedial programs in the basic skill areas.
4. Enrichment projects to overcome cultural impoverishment, enhance motivation, and "widen the horizons" of pupils from depressed areas.
5. Special guidance programs to extend counseling and therapy services to disadvantaged pupils and their parents. Parent education—which interprets the educational needs and potential of disadvantaged children to their parents—is gaining significance as a guidance function.

6. Individual and small-group tutoring programs with professionals, paraprofessionals, and volunteers of all kinds to enhance the individual's self-concept as well as to provide him with personal remedial assistance.
7. Lengthening of the school day and year and extension of activities into the community and neighborhood.
8. Pre-service and in-service teacher training to deepen teachers' understanding of the life-styles and growth patterns of children from depressed areas, and to test and to improve teaching strategies and methods which might work with low-income children.
9. Development of materials to involve the disadvantaged child, to extend his cognitive development, and to provide needed remedial assistance.
10. Work-study and continuation programs involving work exploration, on-the-job training, and subsidized work experience. Continuing education, especially for the sixteen- to twenty-one-year-olds, resulting in new kinds of school programs.
11. Additional staff assigned to schools in depressed areas and adaptation of staff utilization patterns, including as many as a dozen "special service personnel" to augment regular faculty positions in schools with disadvantaged pupils.
12. Programs designed to bring individuals into college and other post-secondary school programs through nonstandard avenues.
13. Recruitment and training of classroom and school aides who perform a variety of services and activities which enable teachers to work in other ways with pupils and the community.

The education of culturally and economically deprived students in the secondary schools will continue to receive a great deal of attention and priority in the future. Furthermore, the social studies program will be largely responsible for instilling the objectives of American education within this segment of the school's population, thus attempting to reduce the degree of cultural disadvantagement among the nation's populace. Due largely to the characteristics of urbanization which have been discussed above, prospective social studies teachers who are considering a career in the urban area, as well as experienced teachers of urban students, must make every effort to attain the best possible comprehension of the forces that have created culturally disadvantaged youth and what educational programs are being advanced to alleviate this negative connotation which is applied to a substantial proportion of the nation's youth.

ENVIRONMENTAL CONTROL AND THE HUMAN ECOSYSTEM

The adequacy of the nation's resource base is comparable to peace, nuclear holocaust, and population control as a crucial issue of our time and of the future. It has direct implications for both the optimum size of our population and the standard of living which that population might enjoy. However, only recently have Americans been confronted with such assumptions as that millions of inhabitants of the United States may be on the verge of starvation within the foreseeable future, that the nation's global position of power and prestige may plunge drastically as a result of overconsumption of nonreservable resources, that a substantial drop in the material standard of living is inevitable unless the natural rate of population increase is significantly curbed, and even extreme positions such as that city dwellers will die from a lack of oxygen and water in our major urban areas unless drastic action is taken to significantly reduce air and water pollution. These and countless other issues are involved in the debate over the ability of the natural environment to support humanity. Again, the problems and prospects related to this contemporary issue are directly within the domain of the secondary social studies curriculum.

Population and Resource Utilization

At one time or another, nearly all social studies teachers have asked questions somewhat like: How many people is the earth or a particular nation capable of supporting? Obviously, the populations of all biological species are limited by their environmental capabilities and mankind is no exception. This planet has been appropriately termed "Spaceship Earth." It possesses a closed system as far as usable materials or resources are concerned. Regardless of continued space exploration there is no scientific evidence to support the belief that we can exploit and import resources from other planets in the solar system for use on earth. Earth is our natural habitat and probably will continue as long as the human species survives. Thus, its environmental potentialities in terms of its population must continually be considered and reevaluated.[28]

The availability of resources at any time is the result of the interactions among the type and extent of man's requirements, the physical occurrence of the resource, and the means of producing it. Furthermore, man's resource requirements depend, among other things, on the absolute size, distribution, and density of populations. In global perspective man is confronted with a rapidly expanding population increase into particular regions. Within such areas, there are further concentrations within urban and metropolitan conurbations. While each human being requires an increase of basic environmental elements such as water, food, clothing, shelter, space, and oxygen, he also requires more. How much more depends upon individual desires and abilities. Thus, it is the responsibility of the social studies instructor to point out that population patterns and concentrations attain greatest significance when the natural and cultural environments are considered in flexible terms. A most significant principle is that a "resource" may be considered less a physical substance than a cultural or technological achievement. This applies not only to mineral resources, but also to water, soil, vegetation, climate, as well as location. Although the natural habitat sets limits upon human activities and ambitions, man is capable of imposing his will upon the environment and creating resources. Resources, then, have reference only to man. But man is not constant, and human changes are accompanied by changes in what constitutes a resource or what man depends on.

The human abilities and skills necessary for the development and utilization of the natural environment to supply the needs of man vary significantly on a global basis. As is noted in a later part of this discussion, most of today's technologically less-advanced societies are not economically underdeveloped or overpopulated because they do not possess natural resources. To the contrary, most of these nations are well endowed with a natural resource base but simply do not possess the education, the human skill and ability, or the capital to exploit and develop their resources. Thus, it is extremely difficult for these nations to become technologically developed and raise living standards for their people. On the other hand, many technologically advanced nations possess so much human skill and capital and have developed resources, economies, and living standards to such a scientific and sophisticated level that they appear to be in danger of depleting their existing resource base and as a result their level of technological achievement and their standards of living.

Population, Resources, and Environment
in the United States

As noted above, the current population of the United States is approximately 208 million, increasing to a total of 300 million or more in 28 years, or by the year 2000. In direct reference to this phenomenal increase, one noted expert on the relationship between man and his environment recently made the following statement: "Each American has roughly 50 times the negative impact on the earth's life-support systems as the average citizen of India. . . . Clearly population growth among Americans is much more serious than population growth in underdeveloped countries."[29] Such a view is exemplary of the emotional nature of the population pressure-resource availability question. As with all other major domestic topics, there exist two sides to the issue. Although the weight of evidence as presented through the mass media and such organizations as the Planned Parenthood-World Population Federation supports the assumption that the United States is in serious danger of becoming overpopulated in relation to its resource capabilities for maintaining its global power position and extremely high living standard, there exists another point of view which suggests that such a dire situation does not and will not exist during the foreseeable future. In contrast to those who predict a population explosion with tragic economic, political, and social consequences unless the natural population increase is stabilized, the latter philosophy makes no such negative predictions and foresees no need to curb population growth in the United States. For this reason, it is the primary responsibility of the social studies instructor to give adequate consideration to both schools of thought.

THEORETICAL VIEWS CONCERNING POPULATION INCREASE AND RESOURCE UTILIZATION IN UNITED STATES

Views Expressed by Those Who Consider the United States Overpopulated

With a current population of approximately 208 million and a projected increase totaling 300 million by the end of the century, there is a great deal of support among influential segments of American society today that the United States is in danger of becoming seriously overpopulated in terms of resource depletion. The answer to this problem as expounded by these groups is to curb population growth immediately by reducing the natural rate of population growth.

While the United States has only about 6 percent of the world's population, it consumes about 40 percent of the world's output of raw materials (not including food). This privileged resource position cannot continue if the economic gap is ever to be closed or even significantly narrowed.[30] For purposes of this discussion, let us assume that between now and the year 2000 the developing countries register a considerably more rapid rate of income gain than the United States, resulting in a substantial narrowing of the per capita income gap. Let us further assume that the result of this trend is a global per capita level of consumption which, by the year 2000, equals that of the United States today. Finally, let us further pursue this argument and assume that the population of the world in the year 2000 fulfills only a most conservative demographic projection: 5 billion people.[31]

To discuss a time only 28 years in the future when the entire world has reached an average level of prosperity equal to that of the United States today may seem extremely optimistic. Yet these two hypotheses together provide a useful tool for coldly examining the dream of a more equitable world—a world in which the income gap between the well-fed and hungry nations has been narrowed. The effect of this model projection is to create a worldwide level of consumption by the end of the century which will be 25 times greater than the U.S. level today. As a result, the degree of environmental pollution and the global drain on resources will be many times greater than those imposed by the United States presently. Advocates of the overpopulation thesis ask us to consider the environmental and geopolitical consequences of a successful effort to narrow the economic gap while U.S. levels of consumption and global population continue to increase. The question is not whether we can somehow survive the coming human deluge. Rather, it is whether, given our standard of consumption and our dream of economic justice, even a "low" total of 5 billion people by the end of this century may not be intolerably high.[32]

The relativity involved in support of a problem of overpopulation in the United States, however, must be introduced by social studies teachers. In Malthusian terms,[33] the claim that the United States has a population problem is difficult to support at the present time. Our population is not pressing upon the domestic food supply. The nation, so far, is not threatened with what Malthus referred to as the "positive checks" on population growth of famine or pestilence, and the third positive check—war—has a dynamic which, for the United States, is entirely independent of internal population pressures. The question whether this country has a population problem turns on a very different set of factors than those envisioned by Thomas Malthus. Instead, overpopulation in the United States is closely related to the quality and safety of our natural environment and social surroundings. The basic question, therefore, is whether our natural and cultural environments are significantly threatened by the nation's natural rate of population increase.

Urbanization and the Environmental Crisis

The locational shifts recorded by the 1970 census deepened the concern of biologists, conservationists, economists, and politicians that the U.S. population was becoming drastically "unbalanced." Typical projections regarding this shift indicated that by the year 2000, 85 percent of the nation's population of 300 million will be urban. Social studies teachers should make it clear that those who support the view that the United States has a definite population problem emphasize that the nation is confronted with a problem in the distribution and density of its population regardless of policies to control its overall size. "Assuming that the trends continue unabated, most of the U.S. population increase over the next few decades will be concentrated in the 12 largest regions. . . . These trends have led to a prevalent sense of gloom for the future of both urban and rural America. It means that hundreds of small American communities will continue to lose young people and that the large metropolitian areas, already burdened with social and fiscal problems and characterized by fragmentation of governmental responsibility, may attain a size at which they will be socially intolerable, politically unmanageable, and economically inefficient."[34]

This unabated trend toward urbanization resulted in a most comprehensive government statement on population distribution issued by the National Goals Research Staff and entitled *Toward Balanced Growth*.[35] This report identified three strategies toward increasing urbanization: (1) generating growth in underpopulated rural areas; (2) generating growth in existing small towns and cities in nonmetropolitan areas; and (3) creating new cities outside the large metropolitan regions. Thus, an overpopulation problem in the United States based upon the current urban distribution was clearly established.

Zero Population Growth in the United States

Closely related to the problem of urban overpopulation, is the concept of zero population growth, which is receiving a great deal of support from several influential agencies which are committed to reducing the natural rate of population growth in the United States. Recently, one such agency, the Population Reference Bureau, emphasized that a wave of women in the United States had begun to flood the prime reproductive ages of 20-29, and that this trend might offset the drop in age-specific fertility. According to this report in

1960 there were only 11 million women aged 20-29; by 1980 there will be nearly twice as many (about 20 million).[36] This population bulge is made up of the children of the post-World War II baby boom.

The objective of the overpopulation thesis, then, is to achieve what is referred to as zero population growth as soon as possible. Zero population growth equals a two-child family, since under current conditions of infant mortality in the United States, an average of about 2.1 children per female would, in a few decades, result in a stable population.[37]

The basic arguments for achieving zero population growth run along the following lines of thought. There appears to be only one viable approach to the population problem in the United States. This is the long tedious route of encouraging Americans to moderate their basic attitudes toward large families. Rather than idealizing large families and creating them, small (two-children) families should become the ideal. Furthermore, instead of promoting forms of economic growth which will increasingly pollute our natural environment, we must insist that we clean up as we go no matter what the cost. Instead of measuring our material welfare by the amount of our consumption, the nation must become deeply concerned about enhancing the quality of life in its various forms.

It has been suggested that "a change in the attitudes of individuals is the key to population control and to many other measures necessary for the amelioration of the population-environmental crises."[38] Indeed, former President Dwight D. Eisenhower remarked in 1968: "Once, as President, I thought and said that birth control was not the business of our Federal Government. The facts changed my mind . . . I have come to believe that the population explosion is the world's most critical problem."[39]

Opposition to Population Control in the United States

Due to the controversial nature of the population-environmental control issue, social studies teachers must present the viewpoint (although a minority view) of those who do not feel that the United States is confronted with an overpopulation problem or that controlling population growth will reduce resource depletion and environmental pollution. Furthermore, this group does not feel that our natural environment is in danger of being destructively exploited to the point of not being able to support a continued economic and technological growth.

The basic arguments set forth by the opponents of population control involve the expenditure of capital to alter the natural environment, thus improving its ability to support greater densities of population and reordering the nation's fiscal spending priorities and placing more emphasis upon improving the human, economic, and social condition of many of the nation's citizens. Giving more attention to both the natural and human environment, rather than reducing and controlling the natural rate of population increase is, in their view, the answer to the population question.

The people who feel that the overpopulation-environmental issue has been exploited place great faith in the ability and potentials of advanced technology. For instance, they argue that an analysis of modern technologies' potential makes it obvious that the earth's ability to produce adequate food supplies need no longer be the primary factor in limiting population growth. One national expert on population-environmental problems has recently pointed out that nearly 10 percent of the land area of the earth, or about 3.5 billion acres, is under cultivation. Continuing, he suggests that with sufficient capital expenditure to improve the natural environment some 15 billion acres of land could be considered arable, or more than four times the present area.[40] In addition to increasing the arable area, crop yields may also be increased by applying technology and capital investment in chemical fertilizers, pesticides, herbicides, irrigation, and the development of new high-yield hybrids.[41]

Colin Clark, the director of the Agricultural Economics Research Institute of Oxford and an exponent of increasing populations, has estimated that by applying technological capabilities on the natural environment equivalent to that of Japanese standards of agriculture, nearly 30 billion people could be supported on a caloric standard of western Europe. Further, Mr. Clark estimates that 100 billion persons could be supported on earth if they were content with the characteristics of the Japanese diet.[42]

In essence, this view holds that the United States, with a current population of 208 million and a projected increase to 300 million by the turn of the century will pose absolutely no environmental or social problem. This assumption is based upon the highly sophisticated technological capability and the enormous amount of investment capital that the nation possesses. The major change that must be made, in the view of this group, is not to promote a national policy to reduce the natural rate of population increase in the United States but, rather, to encourage fiscal spending policies which will place a priority upon developing the nation's environmental potential and improving the social and economic standard of the population. This group firmly believes that a healthy economy depends upon a steadily increasing population and that if the nation's investment capital is directed toward constantly improving the human condition and developing the environmental potential of the United States, a population problem based upon absolute numbers will become less of a negative issue.

STUDENT DISSENT AND YOUTH SUBCULTURE: SIGNIFICANCE FOR SOCIAL EDUCATION

Student Dissent and Political Socialization

By the very nature of both the content and the ultimate objectives of social studies instruction, the phenomenon of student dissent is of particular significance to secondary social studies instructors. If instilling youth with a mode of inquiry to reflect upon and critically analyze the social, economic, and political aspects of the human condition is a basic goal of social education in the United States, then active student dissent must be encouraged both in and out of the classroom.

However, social studies teachers do have the responsibility to channel this dissent in a positive direction. It should be emphasized throughout the study of the various social studies subjects that dissent has and continues to be the foundation of our democratic system. Additionally, students should understand that dissent is vital to the democratic process and that laws prohibiting dissent or the right to dissent are among the most negative characteristics of a totalitarian form of government. Furthermore, the social studies instructor should underscore that there is a fine line between conscientious and sincere dissent, on the one hand, and negative or derogatory dissent, on the other. It should be emphasized that the only guides to dissent that a student possesses are his intellectual background and knowledge of the issue and his sincerity and commitment to the particular condition in question.

Much of the positive student dissent throughout the nation, in the opinion of many educators, is the result of teaching students to inquire into contemporary socioeconomic issues rather than simply accept someone's opinion, to reflect in relative rather than absolute thought, and to demonstrate an active rather than passive attitude toward domestic and international affairs. Social studies teachers must be aware that secondary students can no longer be taken for granted. When discussing issues of a controversial nature, it is of little significance if the majority of students will continue to remain content, passive, and silent, for a determined minority of conscientious students has caused social studies educators as well as other elements in society to examine traditional priorities, values, and procedures. No curriculum has as much to contribute to sincere dissent and positive change in the American human condition as the secondary social studies program.

One of the foremost objectives of social studies instruction is that of political socialization. Two of the basic purposes of political socialization in secondary social studies instruction are to form student attitudes toward their political system and to encourage active student participation in political affairs. For these reasons, student participation and conscientious dissent should be viewed as positive outcomes of social studies instruction which has accomplished one of its major objectives in a democratic society.

CHAPTER 4

Teaching Contemporary International Issues: Interdisciplinary Themes

The second major area of concern for the secondary social studies curriculum is that of promoting education for international understanding. Similarly, most contemporary international issues or those areas of global concern that will have lasting significance during the lifetime of today's students, are cross-disciplinary in nature. Thus, they cannot be assigned to any specific subject in the secondary curriculum, but, rather, have significance for most of the subject areas and, therefore, must be integrated within the existing curricular framework. Throughout the first two major international issues to be considered in the following discussion—Teaching Global Population Dynamics and Introducing the Study of Communism and Communistic Societies—an attempt will be made to introduce and show how the inquiry approach might be utilized in social studies instruction at the secondary level.

TEACHING GLOBAL POPULATION DYNAMICS*

Population pressure and low living standards might be considered the most explosive forces in the modern world. Unless the problem of matching mankind and food production is solved, the world faces chaos in the form of not only hunger, poverty, and disease, but of bitterness, conflict, and violence of global proportions. During the past three centuries world population has increased about fourfold.

*Material in this section was originally published under the title "Introducing the World Population Crises to Secondary Social Studies Classes: An Inquiry-Oriented Instructional Strategy," by Randall C. Anderson, *Social Education,* Vol. 34, No. 1 (January, 1970).

The growth over the past half-century has been nearly one billion. Obviously, this recent demographic expansion is unprecedented in human history. The current trend, long continued, is viewed by many as "calamitous." Expressing the opposite thesis concerning global population dynamics are formidable religious organizations and political ideologists who vigorously denounce the threat of a world demographic crisis. These latter groups, although representing a minority view, expound the assumption that outdated and backward social, economic, and political institutions, rather than absolute numbers of people, are responsible for the negative human condition which currently exists throughout much of the world. Similar to other subjects of a controversial nature, it is vital that social studies teachers encourage students to explore both points of view regarding population growth.

Implementing the Inquiry Approach

The following discussion represents an instructional strategy for introducing the skills of critical analysis to the consideration of a vital contemporary issue for the purpose of improving students' ability to apply the inquiry method and reflect upon social issues in a relative rather than purely descriptive context. At the conclusion of each of the four major themes concerning global population dynamics in this discussion, there are suggestions for "Assumptions for Student Analysis." For classroom purposes, each theme and the accompanying assumptions might be reproduced and presented to the entire class, which should motivate spontaneous and unstructured discussion and debate.

Global Demographic Characteristics and Regional Distribution

A hypothetical "world population clock" — similar to the one that the Census Bureau uses in Washington to keep track of U.S. population growth — would show that, on the average, 3.9 babies were born every second in 1971 while just under 1.7 people died. On a yearly basis about 127 million births occur, 55 million people die, leaving some 72 million human beings added to the world's population. This amounts to a natural rate of increase of 2.2 persons per second, 132 per minute, 7,900 per hour, 190,000 per day, and over 1.3 million a week. The "clock" would have revealed a world population of nearly 3.7 billion by January, 1972; an increase of more than 72 million more than the growth during the year 1970.[1] Forty years ago, the world population was increasing by only 20 million annually.

The natural rate of population growth is the excess of births over deaths, expressed in percentage terms. Currently, world population is increasing at about 2.1-2.2 percent annually, with regional growth rates ranging from less than 1 percent for northwestern Europe to between 3.4-4.5 for parts of Latin America and Africa. The global demographic rate has been moving upward for the past 2,000 years. It is estimated that it took some 600,000 years for mankind to reach the billion mark. This figure was reached early in the 1800s. The 2 billion mark was surpassed in 1930. Indeed, it took only 50 years, from 1900 (1.5 billion) to 1950 (2.5 billion), to add one billion more people. Presently, the world is growing at the rate of a billion people in only 15 years. World population is expected to pass the 4 billion mark by 1975 and nearly double again to approximately 7.5 billion during the next 25 years, or by the year 2000. Thus, at the present rate of growth, the world population would reach 100 billion in less than 200 years — and more than 3,000 billion in less than 500 years. In about 1,700 years, unless there were migrations to other planets, the weight of humanity will exceed the weight of the planet earth.[2]

Globally, the world's people are divided into two major demographic groups. (1) The technologically advanced nations, comprising western Europe, the Soviet Union, Anglo-America, Australia, New Zealand, and Japan — these countries have low birth rates (from 17 to 25 per 1,000) in approximate balance with low death rates (8 to 12 per 1,000). Consequently, they have a slow rate of population growth. The total population of this sector of the world is nearly a billion. (2) The developing nations of Asia, Latin America, and Africa have a total population approaching 2.6 billion people. These countries have continuing high rates of population growth, with birth rates ranging from 39 to over 50 per 1,000 in population and with declining death rates that range from 10 to over 30 per 1,000 in some African countries. The rate of population growth is still rising in these regions of economic scarcity while the urbanized-industrialized nations have control of their fertility pattern. A basic concept for student awareness is that the reduced rate of population growth in these advanced nations is due to what is referred to as the "demographic transition" — the transition from a high-birth-rate, high-death-rate culture (with low living standards) to a low-birth-rate, low-death-rate culture (with higher living standards). This transition in the advanced nations began early in the nineteenth century with a steady decline in both the death rate and the birth rate.

The apparent tragedy, however, is portrayed by recent United Nations estimates which revealed that more than 85 percent of the population increase for the remainder of this century and throughout the twenty-first century will be experienced by the developing so-

societies of Asia, Africa, and Latin America.[3] With regard to Asia, one half of the world's 2 billion people lived in this continent in 1930. Today, Asia contains about 2 billion people, or over 57 percent of the world's total population. On the basis of the projected trends, East, South and Southeast Asia will contain over 4.5 billion people in 2000, or approximately 62 percent of the total.[4] In terms of absolute numerical gains, Asia, with her huge population base, far exceeds any other major region. Latin America's high rate of population increase gives it the dubious distinction of being the most rapidly growing region in the world. Africa ranks after Asia and Europe as the third most populous continent. The five regions into which it is subdivided contain 317 million people. By 2000, Africa's expected population total of 860 million will make it second largest in the world.[5] Sadly enough, no major region in the developing world is now measurably passing through the transitional phase from high to low fertility.

Although there is no general measure of the terms "developed" and "developing," the United Nations reports that, with few exceptions, the level of human reproductivity is the characteristic which best separates the "emerging" from the economically "advanced" countries.[6] The current demographic response in emergent nations is due to the growing imbalance between births and deaths. If birth rates were decreasing as rapidly as death rates, population growth would not be so rapid.[7] However, in developing societies birth rates continue to remain high.

Assumptions for Student Inquiry

1. The current world "population explosion" is the most serious economic, social, or political problem confronting mankind today. It is even more significant than the continued possibility of thermonuclear war.

2. The relatively rapid rate of population increase is not of "world-shaking" importance, since a population distribution map would reveal that most of the earth's land surface, particularly in the developing areas, which are experiencing the most rapid increase, is very sparsely settled or uninhabited altogether.

3. The present rapid rate of population increase is not due to an increase in the birth rate but, rather, is mainly the result of medical technology and sanitation procedures which extend longevity and greatly reduce death rates.

4. The primary reason the developing regions of Africa, Asia, and Latin America are experiencing such a large population increase is not because they are less-developed economically but because they have much greater absolute populations in terms of numbers than do the advanced nations.

5. Due to the widespread availability of antibiotics and other medical achievements the only eventual answer to global population crises is either full-scale nuclear war or worldwide famine.

Theoretical Views Concerning Population Growth

All organisms must adapt to their environment or perish. Man is confronted with the ominous paradox that as he develops his cultural environment to a higher degree he becomes increasingly vulnerable to catastrophe. A specific example is the antithesis between the modern means to assure a long and healthy life and the danger that mankind will be smothered by its own numbers. One demographer has gone so far as to suggest that man will have multiplied himself out of space by the year 2025, or as he puts it — Doomsday![8] This tragic view is supported by those who feel that the future of much of Latin America, Africa, and Asia is destined to include a mounting increase of civil tensions, violence, and armed revolution as the food scarcity becomes more acute. The timetable of food shortages will vary from nation to nation, but it has been predicted that by 1975 the "time of famines"[9] will have begun on a global scale.

Since the beginning of the nineteenth century, there have been two opposing philosophical views concerning population growth. These divergent theories have arisen from the adherents of Malthus, Marx, and Roman Catholicism. In 1798 the British social economist Thomas Malthus first formulated his general laws of population growth. His basic premise was that population tends to increase faster than the means of subsistence and, therefore, must be controlled either by checking the rate of reproduction or by maintaining high death rates. Sooner or later there must come a time when population greatly exceeds the supply of food and the other necessary commodities of life, and thus must be reduced by either "positive" or "preventive" checks. Until the mid-nineteenth century, widespread famine, disease, and war were the main "positive checks" that kept a population balanced with the means of subsistence. In addition, there were "preventive" or "prudential checks" such as the postponement of marriage and continence which resulted in a decline of the birth rate.[10]

Expressing the opposite position concerning the demographic problems of emergent nations are the communist ideologists who remain fanatically opposed to the Malthusian principles and are scornful of any talk of population pressure on the means of subsistence, which they consider to be "cannibalistic." The contemporary communist view is the result of the theories of Karl Marx (1818-83), whose basic thesis was diametrically opposed to that of Malthus. According to the Marxist-Leninist, it was—and currently is—the antiquated social systems (namely, extreme forms of capitalism) under which two-thirds of the world's population live which cause low living standards rather than the absolute population numbers or high rate of natural increase in the less-developed nations. For Marx, the overthrow of capitalism was a prerequisite to all social betterment, and the solution to the population problem would be automatic under socialist economic institutions. Experience, however, has repudiated the sweeping statements of both Malthus and Marx. Indeed, birth control is widely practiced in the Soviet Union and is encouraged by the People's Republic of China, ostensibly to protect the health of mothers[11]—in spite of official adherence to Marxist doctrine.

In addition to the Marxist-Leninist theorists the second of the major opponents of effective preventive population checks is Roman Catholicism. The Catholic church, which long sponsored an "expansionist" policy regarding human reproduction, continues to officially oppose programs for the dissemination of birth control information. Catholic opposition to birth control is especially difficult to understand and to combat because it embraces such diverse and conflicting interpretations. The essence of the contemporary Catholic view seems to be that man needs material wealth, but not at the price of losing his soul.[12]

Assumptions for Student Inquiry

1. The continual discussion of the fear of overpopulation or a "population explosion" in developing countries is the result of capitalistic propaganda expounded by Western demographers, economists, and sociologists in an attempt to explain the tragically low living standard in the developing world.

2. An additional reason for west European and Anglo-American concern about the great population increases in the non-Western world is based upon the racial issues. Since the vast majority of the world's expanding population is non-white, the white, or Caucasian, race which predominates in western Europe and North America is rapidly becoming the world's smallest racial minority group.

3. If the people in developing nations would overthrow their existing antiquated economic and political systems there would be no fear of overpopulation, since greater numbers of people would automatically increase economic development, resulting in a higher living standard for all people residing in these areas.

4. The adoption by developing nations of a complete socialistic economic and political system based upon the principle of central economic planning (that is, communism) would remove the problem of population pressure and low living standards, since a socialistic system would provide for a more equal distribution of the nation's resources and wealth than exists under the present quasi-capitalistic systems in these areas.

5. Outdated religious beliefs and irrational political ideology are the two primary reasons for the current population crises which exist throughout over two-thirds of the modern world.

6. Even though the world's communist regimes are quick to denounce or hesitate to even recognize the existence of overpopulation in the developing nations on ideological grounds, they are very much concerned about the problem in actuality and encourage the reduction of the natural rate of population increase within their own nations through various methods, including abortion, contraception, and postponement of marriage.

7. Catholic opposition to birth control programs in emerging nations, particularly in Latin America and the Caribbean, continues to retard the potential contribution that might be made by international organizations, such as the United Nations, in their efforts to reduce population growth rates in these areas.

8. The Malthusian assumption of population growth expressed in 1798 is more valid today for two-thirds of the world's people than ever before, since during the next 15 to 20 years world population will have increased to the point where mankind will destroy himself through famine, starvation, and wars for the control of food-producing areas.

Significance of the Uninhabited Earth: Land and Water

An examination of a world population map will disclose two highly significant characteristics: The arrangement of people on earth is very uneven and most of the earth's surface remains relatively uninhabited. A major generalization for student awareness is that the global pattern of population distribution reflects the opportunities for human groups to make a living.[13] Presently, more than 75 percent of the world's 3.5 billion people is concentrated in three major clusters comprising approximately 20 percent of the earth's land area (monsoon Asia, western and northwestern Europe, and eastern Anglo-America) while nearly half of the earth's surface is inhabited by less than one person per square mile.[14]

One of the foremost questions currently confronting mankind involves the potential capacity of the remaining 75-plus percent of the earth's land area, which remains largely uninhabited due to extreme environmental limitations, to support larger population densities. The chief deterrents to increasing food production, and thus the human "carrying capacity" in these marginal areas, are the high cost of constructing agricultural and technological facilities as well as the factor of cultural isolation. In addition, expanding cities utilize more and more territory and usually the most potentially arable areas. An effective technique for motivating student inquiry concerning the world's environmentally negative regions involves a discussion of the communist ideological view toward the natural environment. The Marxist believes that under communism mankind will have available the necessary capital and technical ability to alter, reconstruct, or overcome the harsh nature of any marginal environment. Furthermore, the communist ideologists claim that the Western philosophy is one of environmental determinism, which is used simply as an excuse to explain the abominable human condition existing in many of the world's developing areas.

With regard to the more than 75 percent of the earth's surface which is comprised of water, so far the oceans, seas, and major lakes have basically retained the nature of a hunting and gathering ground. Nevertheless, the potential of the ocean's depth is infinite as a resource for food. With better knowledge of aquatic ecology, it should be possible to manipulate the oceans as commercial farmers do their environments: select the best habitat for each useful fish species, breed better strains, and provide more plankton for feeding. But all of this must wait until the intensive oceanographic research now getting under way can lay a sound foundation for the agricultural development of the sea.

Assumptions for Student Inquiry

1. If the capital wealth and technological abilities of mankind would be directed toward improving the productivity of the 70 to 75 percent of the earth's land surface which is presently considered environmentally marginal or incapable of supporting large numbers of people, most of whom exist in 20 to 25 percent of the earth's land surface, the problem of world overpopulation would cease to exist.
2. The arable areas of the earth's surface have been settled and there are no more regions into which mankind may expand that are environmentally capable of producing enough food to support capital investment and technical ability.
3. There is no need to invest capital and technology to expand the world's arable area. The valid solution to increasing food production is to expand the effort on intensifying production in the

existing arable regions and thus increase crop yields.

4. Western nations, as an excuse for not investing capital in marginal areas of the world to increase food production, use the concept of environmental determinism, or the impossibility of improving extreme environmental limitations, to explain why two-thirds of humanity exist at bare subsistence levels.

5. Contrary to communist ideological pronouncements regarding environmental reconstruction or improvement, the Western capitalistic nations have done much more to increase the human "carrying capacity" of marginal areas of their countries than have the communist nations.

6. Unless the potential of the earth's oceans and seas is realized as a food-producing area in the near future, there is little hope of adequately feeding the world's people by the year 2000.

7. The foremost problems in developing nations are not absolute numbers of people nor high natural rates of increase but, rather, the unwillingness of small, wealthy elite groups to provide capital investment for irrigation, conservation, agricultural education, and mechanization to improve the productive capacity of marginal but potentially arable land.

8. By the year 2000 the map of world population distribution will appear very uneven, much as it does today, with 20 to 25 percent of the land area being heavily populated and 70 to 75 percent either sparsely or entirely uninhabited. There will be one major difference, however; the currently dense population clusters will contain even higher population concentrations than they do today.

Population Increase, Birth Control, and Family Planning

Practically all of the population growth of modern times has been due to the decline of death rates before the decline of birth rates. The reasons for the delayed decline of fertility are mainly social in character. Basically, they center upon the fact that many of the causes of early death can be avoided by increases in technology, that is, mobility of food surpluses and use of antibiotics, while the lowering of birth rates involves preliminary changes in social mores before the relatively simple physical prevention of conception will be effectively used by most classes of society. Have students reflect upon the premise that most societies are much more conservative about changing ideology, especially aspects involving religious and moral issues, than they are in changing technology. Most techniques of contraception and abortion, as well as most of the reasons for using such methods, have been in existence for three to five millennia among small upper classes in complex cultures. However, to influence the average individual to use new methods of controlling fertility requires a loosening of the entire social fabric, which historically has made reproduction the easiest way for the average person to attain social prestige.

In cultures that have attained modern population control, the propaganda in support of new contraceptive devices may have helped to spread the idea of family limitation but cannot be considered as the only reason for the adoption of planned parenthood. For example, there have been significant factors which have promoted family limitation in cities to a greater extent than in the rural areas. Family life in urban areas is less cohesive because family members participate in other institutions and have a broader range of outside contacts. The decline in the birth rate has always been closely associated with the process of urbanization and the employment of women outside the home. Furthermore, in comparison to rural youth, children in cities are usually regarded as economic liabilities, since urban youth contribute relatively little to the family income. Finally, the spirit of individuality prevailing in the city is greater than in the conservative countryside.[15]

No one has yet devised universally acceptable contraceptive techniques (although some believe that oral contraception may be one) or devised effective propaganda among people who have an abysmally low living standard. If a systematic population policy toward establishing fertility controls were pushed as rapidly and energetically as public health controls over mortality are being introduced in many countries at present, the modern demographic transition in some of the emerging nations might be accomplished in 50 to 75 years. However, it may take some of the developing societies as long as it took the Europeans to accomplish their vital transition (150 to 200 years).

Some 30 percent of mankind now lives in the high-income, urban-industrial, demographically stable nations. Only a fraction over two children per woman in such societies is needed to maintain a stable population. In the low-income developing countries national fertility has not been reduced substantially, although some minorities have done so. Some five to eight children are still produced per woman, resulting in a population increase of 50 to 100 percent or greater per generation, although only two to three children are necessary to maintain a stable population. The large proportion of the very young is a serious problem for the present and future in the developing nations; it represents an enormous built-in fertility potential. By 1980 in the "have-not" countries there will be nearly twice as many women in the high fertility ages (20-30) as there were in 1965.[16]

In view of the foregoing, it may seem irresponsible to turn to the optimistic side of the picture, but there is such a side of which students must be aware. There is reason to believe that the human numerical problem can be solved by a world fully alert to the inherent dangers of a continued population explosion and willing to devote resources and energy to attacking them. In this hopeful judgment four elements are most significant: (1) the current development of national policies favoring family planning in some 20 to 30 developing countries; (2) the demonstrated public interest in limiting childbearing; (3) the improvement of contraceptive technology; and (4) the fact that for the first time in history several Oriental societies have begun to reduce their birth rates as a result of governmental programs of birth control.[17]

This, then, is the optimistic case for saying that the developing countries can, if they will, bring their rates of population growth to reasonably low levels in the next two or three decades, provided they have the needed assistance from international, governmental, and private agencies in the advanced world. However, it is an illusion to believe that in the developing world at large, progress in spreading birth control among the masses will be easy or swift. Specifically, if the developing nations, during the next 20 to 30 years, can move from their present annual growth rates of 2.5 to 4.5 percent to between 1 and 1.5 percent, the problems will not be solved entirely but the immediate crises will have passed.

Assumptions for Student Inquiry

1. It is immoral for governments, international or national organizations, religious groups, medical personnel, or health officials to influence the individual's reproductive capacity through encouraging the use of birth control techniques regardless of the economic, social, or political consequences which may be involved.
2. All Christians and Jews, if they profess belief in the significance of "life after death" in the Judeo-Christian context, must oppose all forms of artificial birth control or contraception which prevents the creation of human life on earth to enjoy "everlasting life" after death.
3. Although national and international organizations have given a great deal of attention to introducing birth control programs in developing nations during the last several years, very little progress has been made in convincing the masses of the desirability of various contraceptive techniques.

4. The masses of poor people in developing countries are much more interested in birth control programs and are utilizing contraceptive techniques to a much greater extent than the governments and health officials in developing countries are willing to admit.

5. The greater the extent of urban growth in developing nations the more acceptable birth control techniques will become among the majority of the population in these areas.

6. The rapid advances being made in the use of contraceptive technology in developing nations will prevent the "population explosion" from reaching the projected tragic proportions by 2000 and, consequently, will prevent the threat of famine and starvation which is being predicted for the next 10 to 15 years.

7. The problem of overpopulation and hunger in the developing world would have been largely solved by now were it not for the formidable opposition that Roman Catholicism has brought to bear on national and international health organizations.

8. Regardless of attempts being made by governments and other agencies to create effective birth control and family-planning programs, a basic prerequisite is the establishment of universal educational systems in developing nations to promote literacy among the masses.

9. The lack of interest concerning contraception and family planning among the masses in many emerging nations is the fault of the governments in these countries rather than the ignorance or apathy of the people.

10. Abortion should be legalized as a birth control technique by the governments of every nation in the world.

Conclusion

Classroom discussion of the global population crises must be organized around two sharply contrasting themes: one, of almost unrivaled dangers; the other, of new optimism that the problems may be resolved during the remainder of this century. It is difficult to overstate the importance of either theme. The dangers threaten the entire process of modernization among the more than two-thirds of the world's people residing in technologically underdeveloped nations; the development of their political, social, and economic viability; and, ultimately, the prospects for world peace.

INTRODUCING THE STUDY OF COMMUNISM AND COMMUNISTIC SOCIETIES

Teaching about communism in the contemporary world will continue to pose a most formidable task for social studies teachers during the decade of the 1970s as well as the last three decades of the present century. In addition to other dimensions of international tension involving the communist nations with which teachers must attempt to deal effectively, there are such major considerations as the military conflict in Indochina, "wars of national liberation" throughout the developing world, Soviet policy in the Middle East, the Sino-Soviet dispute, Soviet and Chinese political competition in Africa, Latin America, and south Asia, the emergence of a Marxist-Leninist political base in Chile, the change in attitudes between the United States and the People's Republic of China, the continually evolving Soviet-American relationship, and the increasing political divisiveness in eastern Europe.

Basic to the problem of teaching about the role of communism in a global context is that presently more than one-third of the earth's 3.6 billion inhabitants live under some form of communism and that by the end of this century approximately one-half of the earth's seven billion people will be residing under political, economic, and social systems much closer, philosophically, to socialism or communism than to capitalism. What innovative instructional procedures can be designed to better motivate relative thought and inquiry on the part of secondary students so that their generation might be better prepared to comprehend the phenomenon of communism? In education for understanding, international students repeatedly appear to demand some absolute measure for determining if the human condition in a particular culture region is positive or negative or if a specific economic or political system is good or bad. The following approach represents an attempt for teaching skills of critical analysis when studying about the more than one-third of mankind which currently lives under some type of communist political system. Suggested hypotheses designed to promote critical inquiry, independent thought, and the formation of relative generalizations rather than purely descriptive "answers" are presented at the conclusion of each introductory topic of this discussion. These assumptions might be utilized by the teachers during a study of totalitarian systems in government classes as well as during the consideration of communistic and emergent societies in the study of non-Western cultures and world geography.

Communist Ideology in Theory and Practice

For purposes of classroom discussion, communist ideology or Marxism-Leninism may be defined as an established set of beliefs about the universe and the human condition which are officially proclaimed as "unshakable" scientific laws for social development.[18] The instructor should explain that the purpose of ideological theory is to justify specific policies and conditions, both domestic and foreign. However, it is vital that students understand that ideological explanations will often appear strikingly contradictory in relation to actual practice and thus confuse the difficult task for interpreting and understanding communist action or methods, since ideology is constantly reinterpreted or restated to explain a particular condition or policy. Nevertheless, after students are aware of the more obvious differences between communist theory and practice, classroom discussion of communistic societies cannot afford to ignore Marxian theory, so long as it is understood that ideological statements must be discussed in relative rather than absolute terms. For any intelligible comprehension of current ideological pronouncements it is vital for students to understand that the communist ideologists envisioned a revolutionary conflict putting the proletariat, or working class, in opposition to the capitalists, or the ownership class. The outcome of this class struggle would result in a classless social system which would be the genesis of an era of communism with full equality for all members of society.[19]

Assumptions For Student Inquiry

1. A comparison of a utopian communistic society envisioned by Marxist-Leninist ideologists with the development and structure of contemporary society existing in the Soviet Union, eastern Europe, mainland China, North Korea, North Vietnam, and the Republic of Cuba would reveal that none of the "communist" nations have achieved the goal of a classless society or a dictatorship of the proletariat.

4. The prospects of the Soviet Union, mainland China, North Vietnam, and the remainder of the communist nations for ever achieving the ideological synthesis of a communal society or proletarian dictatorship, based upon the principles of Marxism-Leninism, appear to be diminishing rapidly with each passing day.

3. Social or class status in today's communist nations is determined on the basis of a nebulous combination of variables including family background, wealth, and individual influence rather than upon personal ability, knowledge, and initiative as the communist ideologists claim.

4. Social class formation in communist nations based upon party membership, professional status, educational attainment, and personal wealth has perpetuated a more rigid system of class distinction than currently exists in the Western capitalistic world.

5. Communist ideology does not comprise a list of scientific or constant principles or laws for social development but instead the ideology is continually reinterpreted to justify actual policies carried out by communist leaders that at any given moment necessitate a restatement or reinterpretation of the ideology rather than constant ideological principles determining actual policies.

Monolithic Versus Nationalistic Communism

The current form of international communism is described as polycentrism. Indeed, a recent tabulation reveals that there are currently 88 national communist parties recognized by both Western and Soviet authorities.[20] Polycentrism implies that around the two principal ideological centers or nuclei, Soviet Russia and mainland China, there have emerged other communist forces of note, although of different size and varying political importance. An analytical technique for motivating intuitive thought is for students to reflect upon the hypothesis that world communism is a nebulous and divisive political doctrine and that the world has already witnessed the end of a solidified international communist movement or thrust which formerly was directed by the Soviet Union.

What are the basic characteristics of the current pattern of polycentrism among communist nations? The struggle appears to operate on two levels: a conflict of ideas and a conflict of power.[21] In terms of ideas, the issue revolves around a conservative or liberal interpretation of the major doctrines of Marxism-Leninism. The Soviet position appears to hold the middle ground, neither overly violent, nor ready to compromise, while the Chinese ideologists continue to expound an extremely militant attitude. Regarding power, students might analyze the view that the Sino-Soviet ideological conflict centers upon the following division of the world's communist parties: on one side of the fundamental split are the traditionalists, loyal to the Chinese position, who seek to manipulate the movement by strengthening its organizational discipline and functional cohesion around a worldwide communist movement; on the other side are the pro-Soviet innovators, who stress national economic development and political socialization while giving only symbolic significance to the international movement.[22]

Assumptions for Student Inquiry

1. There no longer exists a monolithic or "international" communistic movement committed to world domination through military conquest.
2. Regardless of the heated ideological disputes continually being carried on by nations of the various communist "camps," all communist nations are dedicated to the destruction of the capitalistic world either by military means, economic strangulation, internal political subversion, or a combination of these basic approaches.
3. The concept of nationalism and domestic economic development is much more important to each individual communist nation than the strategy of promoting international communistic movements at the expense of the pursuance of their own nationalistic goals.
4. The major communist nations, the Soviet Union and mainland China, will eventually destroy each other militarily, thus removing the threat of a worldwide communist movement from the global scene.
5. Regardless of their ideological disputes, the communist countries will stop short of openly becoming embroiled in large-scale military conflicts with one another.
6. As a result of the extreme nature of the polycentrism existing within the communist world, no single communist power, either the Soviet Union or mainland China, will be able to recapture a complete one-nation control over the entire communist movement.

Technological and Scientific Development

An obvious fact about communistic societies is their rapid achievement in creating an impressive economic base. For instance, teachers should emphasize that in the development of thermonuclear energy, missile and anti-missile systems, and other complex scientific advancements, the USSR appears to be little, if at all, behind the United States, and communist China continues to make rapid progress. Since the inception of the communist regimes in the Soviet Union, mainland China, North Vietnam, and North Korea, the basic objective has been to transform and modernize these economies, to overcome military vulnerability vis-à-vis the capitalistic countries and to improve the human condition. At this point, the instructor should encourage research and discussion within the context of the communist system of centralized economic planning which places priority upon rapid techological advancement rather than upon consumer commodities and services.[23]

In a communist society, the means of economic production (the land, natural resources, factories, transportation systems, banks, retail establishments, etc.) as well as the human resources are owned and regulated not by the private economic sector but by the state.[24] Communist central economic planning means more than achieving broad production targets; it means the deliberate quantitative and qualitative enumeration of thousands of items which are needed in the life of a nation, from hydroelectric production to toothbrushes, from nuclear missile systems to the movie industry.[25]

Assumptions for Student Inquiry

1. The primary reason for the rapid rate of growth in industry, technology, and military capabilities in the Soviet Union, eastern Europe, and mainland China is due to the communist system of central economic planning.
2. A comparison of the levels of technological development in the centrally planned economies of North Vietnam and North Korea would reveal a much more rapid rate of economic growth than in the non-communist nations of South Korea and South Vietnam.
3. The human privation and sacrifice with regard to consumer goods and services, which receive little priority under central economic planning in communist nations, can certainly be justified on the basis of the remarkable achievements in industry and technology.
4. Eventually the system of central planning will provide the populations of communist nations with a living standard that will surpass that enjoyed by the inhabitants of the economically advanced Western nations.
5. The most accurate definition of a communist country is a nation that has adopted a program for national development based upon a system of central planning for all sectors of the economy.

The Socialization of Agriculture and Rural Development

The agrarian sector has always presented a major challenge to the communist regimes, for failure in this area during the early stages of the revolutions might well have spelled disaster. Specifically, the communist governments in the USSR, mainland China, North Vietnam, North Korea, and Cuba inherited a peasant base which comprised approximately four-fifths of the population in these nations. How could subsistence peasants be manipulated to play a significant role in a socialized economy so that the priority objective of rapid technological advancement might be achieved?

Although there have been a variety of interpretations concerning the decisions of communist regimes to collectivize agriculture—the establishment of the collective and state farms in the Soviet Union and the commune system in east Asian communist countries—the basic conclusion involves the policy that the decision to launch the collectivization programs was motivated by the objective of creating an agricultural surplus which could be exported to food-deficient nations. In return, the communist countries would import the where-withal—capital and technical advice—requisite for the promotion of rapid technological development. Prior to any discussion involving agriculture in communist societies, students must achieve an under-standing of the rationale for collectivization. Collectives, state farms and communes would (1) destroy the rural, large landholding class in the rural areas and socialize the illiterate peasantry within a more readily managed collectivist economic framework; (2) they would increase agricultural production through mechanization, large-scale farming, and the use of more scientific methods; (3) they would insure a steady flow of both labor and food to the urban-industrial areas; and (4) the chief virtue of the collective farm system, regardless of the communist nations under consideration, was that the government could collect an agricultural surplus very cheaply.[26]

Assumptions for Student Inquiry

1. In illiterate peasant subsistence economies such as existed in pre-revolutionary Russia, mainland China, North Vietnam, North Korea, and Cuba the establishment of collective farms was necessary before any improvement in agriculture or de-velopment of the rural sector could be achieved.
2. The primary purpose of collectivized agriculture in communist countries is not to increase the production of food and improve the dietary level of the populace. Instead, collective farms are to provide an exportable food surplus for the purpose of insur-ing a source of capital to be used for the exploitation of mineral resources and the rapid development of industry and tech-nology.
3. Without collectivized agriculture the Soviet Union and main-land China could not have attained the rapid and advanced level of technological capability which they currently possess.
4. If the communist governments had not introduced collective farms, state farms, and agricultural communes they would not be continually confronted with serious agricultural problems

and furthermore, these nations could have developed their industrial base much more rapidly.

5. The status of the rural peasants, whether on a Soviet collective or an Asian commune, has not improved since the communist seizure of power. They continue to be virtual serfs controlled by the state with little or no freedom in deciding what crops to plant, acreage allotments, or the monetary rewards they should receive for their labor.

6. The human and material conditions of farm families living on Soviet and east European collectives and Asian communes have improved substantially since the communists came to power.

Cultural Integration, Education, and the Development of Human Resources

The manner in which a government discriminates against particular national minorities is one important indication of its political character. Have students discuss the hypothesis that in all countries, during some historical period, national minorities have been convenient scapegoats, both a target for national fear and failure. In societies where totalitarian elites demand complete commitment to official ideology and where the line between dissent and treason is extremely narrow, cultural, ethnic, and religious diversity is presumed to contain the potential of political opposition.[27]

Cultural Integration under Communism

Every communist country, with the probable exception of Albania, East Germany, and Poland has a serious nationality problem. The Soviet Union, of all the communist nations, has the most extensive problem of cultural heterogenity: a complex demographic mosaic of more than 100 distinct nationality or ethnic groups speaking more than 100 different languages and practicing a variety of religions. While the goal of the Soviet leadership is a common communist culture, they acknowledge that the obliteration of national distinctions, and especially of language distinctions, would be a considerably longer process than the obliteration of class distinction. In the meantime, the party remains committed to the continued improvement of the cultural and economic conditions of the non-Russian nationality groups (non-Slavic, since the three Slavic ethnic groups, the Great, Little, and White Russians comprise some 75 percent of the total Soviet population). Though the various ethnic groups are permitted to retain their linguistic and cultural identities, their history and traditions are being blended into an all-encompassing Soviet patriotism — the driving force of which is Great Russian nationalism — in order to promote a greater sense of national viability.[28] This policy of cultural integration is referred to as Russification.

China's nationality problem is of a different dimension, since the minority people constitute only 6 percent of the population. They are, nevertheless, a source of official concern, since they inhabit strategic areas amounting to roughly 60 percent of China's total territory, much of which is reputedly rich in industrial resources. Officially, Peking's policy is one of respecting local languages, customs, and religions. However, centralized control has been extended, often militarily (as in Tibet), over the outlying regions of Yuman, Tibet, Sinkiang, and Inner Mongolia, and an active program of populating these areas with Han Chinese has been initiated. The Chinese version of creating cultural integration is referred to as Sinacization.[29]

Educational Development in Communistic Societies

Recognizing that education is the main tool in the development of human resources required to augment the strategic capability of a nation, educational planners in communist nations place extreme priority on the creation of a high-level professional labor force, particularly the training of specialists in science and technology. Indeed, the collectivist objective of "service to the state" is the primary goal of communist educational efforts, while in the West individualism continues to be emphasized. In pursuance of this objective, communist nations integrate educational and manpower policies, in a functional sense, much more closely with economic objectives than other modern technological nations whose policies are based on more pluralistic values.[30]

With regard to the Soviet Union, mainland China, North Vietnam, and North Korea it should be emphasized that the communist regimes inherited economically underdeveloped countries with a corresponding cultural backwardness. Students must understand that when the communist regimes came into existence the vast majority of the population in each of these countries was illiterate peasants existing upon a subsistence agrarian base. These new governments, through the elimination of mass illiteracy and the establishment of a vernacular language, have created a previously nonexistent national awareness which has resulted in rapid technological, political, and cultural development.[31] A basic concept for student awareness is that, without exception, in every communist country mass educational opportunity has increased enormously in comparison to the situation prior to the advent of communism.

Assumptions for Student Inquiry

1. Members of racial majority groups have a better opportunity to preserve their cultural identity, achieve their potential as individuals, and be rewarded more fairly for their accomplishments in communistic than in Western capitalistic societies.
2. There exists much more tension with regard to problems associated with racial and ethnic minority groups in capitalistic nations than in communist countries.
3. Prior to the communist take-over in Soviet Russia, eastern Europe, mainland China, North Korea, North Vietnam, and Cuba the vast majority of the people in these nations had no feeling of loyalty, unity, or cohesion for their nations.
4. As a direct result of the communistic system of education and cultural integration, the vast majority of the populace in communist countries had developed a high degree of nationalism or patriotism for their particular nations.
5. Prior to the communist revolutions in Soviet Russia, mainland China, and Cuba the majority (80 to 90 percent) of the populations was illiterate peasants living at a subsistence level. As a direct result of the communistic system of educational planing, nearly all of the populace (80 to 98 percent) in these countries are literate and enjoy much higher living standards.
6. The only way in which the peasant societies of pre-revolutionary Russia, China, and the remaining communist states could rapidly achieve literacy, cultural cohesion, patriotism, and pride in their nations was to introduce the communistic system.

Communism and Political Socialization

In addition to the ideological and economic characteristics of communist nations, some discussion of the political institutions by which communist parties maintain power is vital. Three organizational activities are linked to communism's contemporary dictatorship —the purge, the secret police, and the indoctrination or propaganda system.

The Purge. The purge system is a continuous and highly organized characteristic of a totalitarian state. By "purge" is meant the physical and political removal of an individual, or a group of people, whom the state considers its enemies or potential enemies. While all dictatorships engage in purges, the communist states have developed and refined this art to the point where the purges have become a steady background feature of a "dictatorship of the proletariat."

The Soviet purges of the mid-thirties had important implications for every Soviet citizen and immensely affected the future of Russia. For an understanding of communism, the overall pattern for the removal of the "class enemies" is of great significance, since the populace of all communist nations have been subjected to purges of a similar nature. These purges had a steady and ever-widening scope; beginning with the arrest of one individual, they broadened to a "runaway" purge which reached frightening proportions. At the opposite end of the scale are the purges which have been administered in post-Stalinist Russia. Today, the usual punishment involves demotion, loss of job, reassignment, or public censure.[32] This more moderate purge system has even penetrated communist China and eastern Europe. However, there is considerable evidence that events accompanying "The Great Proletarian Cultural Revolution,"[33] which has been continuing in China since 1966, are tragically reminiscent of the mass exterminations of Stalinist Russia.

Communist Indoctrination. Indoctrination, or propaganda, in the broadest sense, is the technique of influencing human thought. Propaganda systems of the twentieth century use every available communication medium from newspapers to radio, television, and motion pictures. The ultimate goal of communist indoctrination is to compel a public acceptance of all major policy decisions of the regime, whether in foreign affairs or in the realm of domestic developments. Total control is the essential feature of the communist propaganda system. There can be no escape from, or compromise with, the absolute "truth" of Marxism-Leninism. In the eyes of the leadership nothing is beyond their scope of control; propaganda will embrace even the most nonpolitical or seemingly neutral activities such as athletics, culture, science, linguistics, and organized religion.[34]

Assumptions for Student Inquiry

1. All developing societies, which, in actuality, are nothing but artificial nations due to the negative factors of cultural pluralism, political instability, and little or no national unity, might well benefit from strict communistic methods of achieving political socialization.
2. The human terror and fear resulting from the utilization of purge and secret police systems in communist nations should be considered positive, since these elements motivate loyalty and rapid accomplishment of national objectives.
3. The existence of the purge, the secret police, the indoctrination system, and the interlocking directorate of party and government simply reflect the insecurity of the various communist

regimes and their fear of being overthrown by the mass revolt unless these instruments of terror exist and are periodically enforced.

4. Communist countries are no less guilty of intense propaganda and indoctrination techniques than were the highly advanced Western nations during their development periods.

5. Sophisticated methods of indoctrination in communist nations are necessary and can be justified on the basis of instilling a feeling of national patriotism among previously illiterate masses who had little regard for national viability.

6. All nations, communist and non-communist, must continue to perpetuate their traditions by constant nationalistic indoctrination through their educational systems and communications media.

Communism and the Human Condition

Although immense changes have occurred in world communism during the last few years, communistic societies continue to retain two fundamental features concerning the human and cultural condition: centralized control over society and a revolutionary change from the previous class structure. In contrast with the voluntary and free nature of Western democratic societies, life under communism is severely restricted—although the methods of control, as previously noted, may vary from time to time.

Rather than stressing the obvious differences between aspects of life existing in the communist and Western nations, present-day living standards should be compared with conditions which existed, for example, in Russia 10, 20, 30, or 50 years ago and in the case of mainland China, North Vietnam, and North Korea with conditions of two decades ago. Evidence is conclusive that the average citizen in any of the communist countries (with the exception of East Germany and Czechoslovakia) has a more abundant selection of consumer goods and services, better living accommodations, educational and employment opportunities, medical services, and recreational facilities than at any time previous to the communist seizure of power. It is much more significant for students to investigate the extent to which life in communist nations has improved somewhat over a relatively short period under extreme conditions rather than to compare present living standards in communistic societies with those existing in the West. Basic to this question is the paradoxical nature of communist economic development. Students must gain an understanding of how these nations can achieve such dramatic scientific advancements when more than half of the populations (excluding several of the east European nations) have no indoor plumbing and where automobiles are still luxuries in nations that have become nuclear powers. Again, the instructor should first encourage discussion of the central planning system which gives top priority to capital goods production rather than to commodities for the consumer market. Second, students should compare the economic policies and resultant social conditions which have existed in today's communist nations with the policies and conditions in developing countries that are attempting to achieve the transition from peasant societies to technological economies within a short time span.

Classroom discussions concerning communistic societies usually center upon the examination of the innumerable restrictions placed upon daily life in these nations.[35] Unfortunately, the lack of individual freedom in communist countries is often magnified by comparing the most rigid restrictions which evolved immediately following the revolutions with the ideal and somewhat utopian civil liberties existing in the Western nations. Prior to making evaluations concerning the degree of limitations imposed upon the masses, students must grasp the significance of examining the term "freedom" in proper perspective. The instructor should explain that the usage is exceedingly relative and that it has divergent meanings for different periods of time within the same nation as well as during the same period between nations.

When students understand the relative implications of personal freedom, they should investigate the assumption that the individual communist citizen (again, with the exception of several east European countries) has never enjoyed a more relaxed political and social atmosphere than he does today. The class should be encouraged to gather evidence concerning the individual's freedom to discuss openly political and economic philosophy, converse with foreign tourists, change jobs, take vacations, and engage in other similar activities. However, human freedoms must be examined in communistic rather than the Western context. Students must gain the perspective that the communist nations are neither tyrannical police states nor nations that have become free in the Western sense of the term.

Assumptions for Student Inquiry

1. Rigid control over the cultural expression of artists, writers, and musicians such as exists in communist states is necessary during the transitional period of nation-building, when the government and party are attempting to replace a rural subsistence class with an urban-technological society.

2. As technical advancement and urbanization proceed in these nations, there will be a definite reduction in the extent of governmental control over individual creativity and cultural expression.
3. Social class distinctions based upon family background, profession or job, party membership, rural or urban residence, or individual wealth or influence are more strictly defined in communist than in Western capitalistic nations.
4. The average wage-earning citizen in a communist nation has a more abundant selection of consumer goods and services (food, clothing, and household items), better living accommodations, educational and employment opportunities, medical services, cultural and recreational facilities than at any time before or since the communist seizure of power.
5. Even though the Soviet Union and the other communist nations are undergoing change, the populace is enjoying greater civil liberty than at any time since the Revolution; the fundamental characteristics of a totalitarian system will continue to be in evidence throughout the foreseeable future.
6. It is not communism as an economic and political system or philosophy that reduces freedom and spontaneous human activity when examined in Western context, but rather, the totalitarian police state methods employed by contemporary communist regimes.

Conclusion

Students should be encouraged to examine the premise that the technological development of communist systems will, in the foreseeable future, give rise to influential interest groups outside the Communist party, mellow totalitarianism, reduce communist rule and produce a meaningful "democratization" of communist countries, thus making them more synonymous with Western democracies.

TEACHING THE SIGNIFICANCE OF DEVELOPING NON-WESTERN SOCIETIES*

Presenting a valid and meaningful appraisal of the underdeveloped, less developed, or emerging nations confronts the social

*Material in this section was originally published under the title "The Role of Human Geography in the Study of Emerging Nations," by R. C. Anderson, Social Education, Vol. 29, No. 6 (October, 1965).

studies teacher with a formidable, but increasingly significant, task. Since the conclusion of World War II, there has been a remarkable awakening of interest in the economically backward areas of the world. Underdeveloped economies are the most extensive on earth. They comprise the whole of Africa and the Middle East (with the exception of South Africa and Israel), parts of Mediterranean Europe, the greater portion of South and Central America, and virtually the whole of Asia outside Soviet Asia, Japan, and parts of Malaysia. These economies support over one-half of the world population (more than 70 percent when the centrally planned economies of the communist bloc are included).[36] The Afro-Asian and Latin American nations will continue to play such a significant role in any consideration of world affairs that students can ill afford to remain ignorant of the many and varied problems facing these nations in their struggle to attain internal stability and international prestige through economic development.

Definition

One of the most difficult tasks of the social studies instructor is that of adequately defining the underdeveloped country and presenting explanations as to why some political entities are categorized as such. It is hard to distinguish between "more developed" and "less developed" nations, since the usage is so loose. Basic to this problem is the factor of relativity, which reduces the significance of the comparative approach as an instructional technique. In a sense, the economy of every country, including the United States, is "underdeveloped," since more can be done to increase its productive power and to improve the well-being of its people. Venezuela's rapid economic development, for instance, contrasts sharply with chaotic conditions in Bolivia and Ecuador. A similar situation is that of the Republic of South Africa's economic and political strength when seen in comparison with the rest of Africa.[37]

Among the numerous criteria used to define levels of economic development are predominant types of productive activity in which a nation's population is engaged. It is possible to classify national economies in four main categories based upon the occupational structure: (1) Highly developed, or industrial, economies support only about 8 percent of the world population. Outside the Western world only Australia and New Zealand could be counted in this group. (2) Semi-developed, or mixed industrial-agricultural, economies support approximately 12 percent of world population. Countries falling within the intermediate range represent every continent and include

Argentina, Venezuela, Uruguay, Japan, South Africa, Finland, Spain, Portugal, and Italy. (3) Underdeveloped, or predominantly agricultural, economies, as previously determined, account for over 50 percent of the people in the free world. (4) Centrally planned economies, which are essentially type 2 or 3, comprise so many special characteristics that they should be considered separately. The Soviet Union, much of eastern Europe, and Cuba could be assigned to the intermediate bloc, while China continues to be classified as underdeveloped. These economies include nearly 30 percent of the world population.[38]

Besides helping to define levels of economic development, elements of the social studies curriculum can be used effectively in teaching about the internal problems of nations. There appear to be several human and economic characteristics that are evident in many underdeveloped countries which are not deviated from to any measurable extent. Nevertheless, it must be emphasized to students that there are exceptions to any model or standard that might be employed. Individual countries have different problems at varying levels of development.

Cultural Patterns

One of the most obvious characteristics of many less developed nations is the extremely uneven distribution of population. In many instances the thinly inhabited regions greatly exceed the area of the more densely populated parts of these nations, especially in Mediterranean and Subsaharan Africa, the Middle East, and China. Students can visualize the wide distributional disparities by examining even a small-scale population map of these regions. They must realize that the pattern of population distribution reflects the opportunities of securing a livelihood. The vast sparsely populated parts of these countries, therefore, contribute very little to the economic growth of the nation, regardless of the resource base for industrialization or the environmental potentials for commercial agriculture.

This spatial arrangement of isolated concentrations of population results in the internal division of the particular political region into two distinct parts which one eminent authority has designated as "total national territory" and "effective national territory."[39] Total national territory, or the political area over which a centralized government claims legal jurisdiction, must be distinguished from effective national territory—that segment of the total area which makes the major contribution to the support of the populace and the nation's economic growth. In Venezuela, the Orinoco Lowland and the Guiana Highlands comprise two-thirds of the national area, but are outside the effective national territory. In Brazil, 90 percent of the population resides within 300 miles of the coast, in less than one-fourth of the total area.[40] The lower Nile Valley and Delta in Egypt, the Mediterranean coastal regions of Algeria, Morocco, and Libya, and the delta areas of the Mekong, Irrawaddy, and Mae Nam rivers in Southeast Asia also represent this internal disparity of population concentration. Obviously, an introduction to this divisive characteristic within these countries should result in student awareness that the areal dimensions of a particular nation are of little significance in determining its poential for economic growth.

Further examination will reveal that the demographic arrangement within the high-density areas of many countries is one of isolated clusters or nodes of population. A result of this isolated or clustered population pattern is the uneven geographic arrangement of transportation systems. The few adequate land transportation routes connect areas of dense population rather than connecting sparsely settled areas, which, of course, would further encourage population redistribution.[41] An interesting map exercise for students is to compare the dense railway network in Europe and the United States with many areas in Africa and Latin America, and to correlate the railroad pattern to population distributions in these four areas. One important conclusion would be that, unlike most areas of Latin America and Africa, transportation systems in many areas of the Western world connect the regions of high and low population densities, thus facilitating the development of the rural areas and small cities.

It should become evident to students from an examination of the population distribution of these nations that the political boundaries usually cut through sparsely inhabited areas. Thinly populated regions, particularly when they are a part of weaker nations, tend to be extremely susceptible to territorial encroachment by stronger neighbors. A vital resource in these areas, such as petroleum, ferrous metal reserves, or arable land, further encourages such intentions or even direct intervention. This situation has been the primary cause of many of the boundary disputes among Latin American nations during the twentieth century.[42] The recurring dispute between the Soviet Union and communist China involving their 4,000-mile "friendship" boundary exemplifies this problem of the vulnerability of a sparsely inhabited border area. Both regimes are actively supporting the migrations of thousands of people, particularly in the contact zones of Sinkiang and the Amur Valley, to discourage possible intrusions.[43] Such disputes will, undoubtedly, become more numerous in Africa and parts of Southeast Asia as a consequence of the recent wave of nationalism that is sweeping across these areas.

Consideration should also be given to an additional aspect of the demographic pattern in less-developed countries—that of the rural-urban ratio.[44] Perhaps the most common and widely accepted criterion applied in differentiating between the "have" and "have not" nations is the percentage of the total population residing in rural areas or actively engaged in agriculture. Although there continues to be considerable confusion in distinguishing urban from rural forms of settlement in many nations, countries which classify 50 percent or more of the populace as rural are generally considered as non-industrial or less advanced economies. Developing economies, therefore, are essentially agricultural economies. Everywhere in these countries the proportion of the working population in agricultural pursuits is very high, reaching about 60 percent in many of the cordilleran states of Latin America, 70 percent in much of East, Southeast, and South Asia, and a still higher percentage in Africa. The danger of using such a rationale without question is illustrated again by the recent spectacular development of Venezuela (where nearly 50 percent of the population is engaged in agricultural activity).[45] A comparison of economic development and the rural-urban ratios of western Europe with the Balkans and Mediterranean Europe will, nevertheless, support the general validity of such a test. Furthermore, the significance that certain governments place upon attaining international economic "status" by having a majority of the population residing in the urban area is exemplified by recent pronouncements of the Soviet regime regarding the results of the 1959 All-Union Census.[46] The main reasons for employing such a classification include the low capitalization of agriculture in the pre-industrial economy, a low level of rural income, and the low productivity of rural laborers.

Students should gain some insight into the problems of the rural populace in the developing countries through a careful examination and interpretation of slides or pictures comparing rural scenes in western Europe and the United States with those in other nations.

Regionalism

Closely associated with the problem of extremely uneven population distribution is the phenomenon of pronounced regionalism so prevalent in many underdeveloped countries. A consideration of underdeveloped areas offers students one of the best opportunities to define regions based upon human criteria and to grasp the significance of the regional concept as it applies to the study of any area of a country.

Peoples in the emerging nations tend to develop stronger attitudes of devotion and loyalty to separate provinces or isolated regions than to their nations. This lack of a widespread feeling of national cohesion or identity, in an extralegal sense, is partly the result of the clustered pattern of human habitation throughout the country and partly a consequence of the fact that the majority of the populace occupies only a small fraction of the total national territory. As previously mentioned, nodes of population are likely to be scattered and separated by a lack of adequate land transportation systems and by environmental barriers, such as mountain ranges, dense forested areas, or expanses of arid or semi-arid land. Isolated groups, therefore, have little immediate contact and develop little interest or knowledge of other peoples, both between widely separated parts of the country and within the heavily populated areas. The absence of national unity is a major part of the problem of political fragmentation which is evidenced throughout much of the underdeveloped world.

An additional aspect of this internal division involves the regional "core"[47] of a nation. This concept implies that one heavily populated area or region is the primary focal point for the diffusion of ideas throughout the country. Core regions coincide with the largest area of dense population, include the largest portion of the nation's economic activity and the political capital, and tend to influence the cultural level throughout the country. Negatively, these core areas have been accused of promoting "regional imperialism" as a result of their inability to distinguish between regional goals and national goals. From earliest times in Mexico, all other regions have been unwilling subordinates to the Federal District.[48] Other prominent examples of regional cores in developing nations include Addis Ababa and Montevideo in Ethiopia and Uruguay, respectively. These areas have acted historically as the nucleus for the development and diffusion of national culture, and they continue to be the dominant regions in this respect. The process of achieving a national awareness — or a nation-state idea among groups of people residing within the same political boundaries — will undoubtedly continue to be hindered by varying degrees of regional centralism.

The Agrarian Population

Fundamentally, there appear to be two related issues confronting the governments of less-developed countries in their attempt to improve human conditions in the rural sector. First, there is the problem of an ever-increasing division between rural and urban employment opportunities and living standards. Second, there is the almost universal opinion that economic development and modernization are synonymous with intensive industrial development and that priorities must be given to industry over agriculture. Both these issues possess definite geographic implications.

The disparity in social conditions that exists between the rural and urban sectors is generally accepted as a result of both the system of landholding and the subsistence level of a majority of the rural inhabitants. Landholding in the non-industrial economies is a problem of extremes which has been characterized as "men without land and land without men."[49] These economies are characterized by large landed estates owned by a relatively small percentage of the population. It is not uncommon for from 5 to 10 percent of the population to hold title to over 80 percent of the arable land.[50] The system of land tenure is regarded as one of the most critical political and social issues in the underdeveloped country.

The subsistence economic level characterizes not only the tenant labor force, but also the majority of sedentary, small landowners and indigenous nomadic groups. Primitive subsistence agriculture, which includes shifting cultivation, nomadic herding, and sedentary intensive productions, is the least commercialized of all agricultural types, and is the most extensive in terms of both number of people and of area in the underdeveloped country. Such an economy is characterized by no specialized production, little commodity exchange, and no commodity surplus. All human energy is consumed in supplying the basic human needs – food and shelter.

Programs of agrarian reform intended to break up the large estates and redistribute more equally the arable land among tenants and small landholders are hindered by several basic problems characteristic of developing societies. The subsistence farmer lacks modern agricultural techniques, the soil is frequently exhausted and eroded, farm implements are antiquated, and chemical fertilizers are either unknown or too expensive. Thus, even though the large landholding system possesses obvious inequalities and its value is exaggerated in the pre-industrial society, perhaps it contributes more to the national economy over the short run than large-scale programs of land redistribution will, particularly since there is some direction and capital investment.

The other aspect of the agrarian problem in underdeveloped nations involves the thesis that rapid and intensive industrialization is the main prerequisite for economic progress and the raising of living standards. Although the differences between advanced and less-advanced countries are complicated, authorities generally agree that industrial complexity is equated with national power and international prestige. In both theory and practice, priority is given even to token industrialization, and the problems of agriculture are generally neglected.

Urbanization

A discussion of city growth in developing countries should enable students to distinguish between "true" urbanization or economic growth reflecting an expansion of non-agricultural activities, as in the United States, and "false" urbanization. Spurious growth, which characterizes urban development in many emerging nations, is mainly the result of a hope on the part of many rural people that a better existence might be attained in the city. Urbanization is outpacing industrialization in these countries.

Currently, a rapid rate of urban growth is one of the most obvious characteristics of the underdeveloped nation. The foremost cause of this accelerated urbanization is the migration from the rural areas which continues to gain momentum in Africa, Asia, and Latin America. Small farmers and tenant laborers, fed up with misery and poverty, rush to the cities in the belief that things will be better. The prospects for securing "guaranteed poverty" seem to be more promising in the city than in the country.

The most tragic result of this human influx into the city is the uncontrolled growth of almost unimaginable slum areas, or "shantytowns," as they are referred to in Latin America. The extreme poverty and complete hopelessness confronting the countless thousands existing in these areas continue to be portrayed and documented in depressing terms. More significant, however, is the apparent lack of any formula to alleviate this ever-increasing problem.

An additional dimension of this problem of urbanization in the underdeveloped country is its unevenness. Existing large cities are experiencing a much more rapid rate of relative growth than smaller cities and towns. Thus, the principle of "high primacy" will continue to characterize urban development in many of these nations. The "primate city" is one in which there is a major concentration of population in one large metropolitan area as compared to the other cities within the country.[51] A "bi-primacy" pattern is said to exist in certain countries where two major cities are experiencing a nearly equal growth. Compared to Asia and Latin America, the rate of growth of urbanization in Africa is relatively small. This is due mainly to the deliberate attempt by white settlers to keep the Africans out of the towns.[52] This situation is rapidly changing throughout much of the continent as a result of the independence movement. Indeed, the problems of urban growth in African nations will become more acute.

Although the primacy concept is not a new phenomenon in national development, it presents several serious problems to governments attempting to broaden economic opportunity. The criticisms of primate cities are many and varied. It has been suggested that they are "parasitic" cities, since they tend to monopolize the skilled and professional people, thereby leaving the rural areas without these services. Paradoxically, in much of Asia, Africa, and Latin America, there is a surplus of unskilled labor in rural sectors, the areas which are most in need of large numbers of skilled personnel, if the environmental potentials are to be realized. As previously mentioned, the migration of these uneducated masses into the cities in search of more tolerable conditions has contributed greatly to the "shantytown" explosion.

On the positive side, the development of urban centers in the major city or cities in underdeveloped countries has contributed significantly to the emergence of a middle class. The growing opportunities for many people to secure salaried annual employment in the growing exchange and commercial city economy will continue to reduce substantially the image of a wealthy minority and the poor masses.

Population Dynamics

In evaluating a nation's potential for technological advancement, students must give consideration to the population base in terms of size, growth, and age structure. Thus, students must understand that unless programs designed to improve a nation's well-being are firmly grounded in these basic demographic facts, they can be seriously undermined. The population of these countries represents their greatest liabilities.

Overpopulation is a major problem confronting the underdeveloped nation. Basic to the problem of population pressure is the high national increase rate being experienced by these nations. In most non-industrial societies the current accelerated population growth is due almost entirely to a reduction of mortality rates, particularly infant mortality. Thus, the natural increase—the excess of births over deaths — accounts for the lion's share of population growth in the less-advanced nation. Usually the first step in aiding the less fortunate peoples of the world is the introduction of preventive medicine and programs of sanitation for the control and eradication of death-dealing diseases. As a result, death rates decrease significantly while birth rates remain extremely high and the population growth rate soars.

By 1971, the world's population was increasing between 2.0 and 2.2 percent annually. Although there is a slight variance in figures, due mainly to incomplete census taking, it is conclusive that the less-developed regions are experiencing a much higher rate of demographic growth than the world average. Specifically, the fastest growing regions are Central America and South America, where the population is increasing at slightly more than 3 percent annually, and will double in only 23 years. In contrast, the population of the United States is increasing at 1.6 percent a year, or slightly below the world average, and will double in approximately 40 years. It is significant, however, that the population of Latin America is now growing more rapidly than that of any other large region at any time in history. In Africa, very little accurate information exists regarding vital demographic statistics. Nevertheless, the highest birth and death rates in the world are probably found in this continent, and indications are that this rate of growth will increase substantially when programs of preventive medicine are implemented on a scale comparative with those in Latin America.

Two out of every three people on earth live in Asia, and nearly five of every six births occur there. The rate of natural increase for most of Asia (excluding Japan, but including India) exceeds 2.2 percent.[53] While this figure is above average, it represents a comparatively low rate of growth in comparison to most of Latin America. Most of the Asian regions, like Africa, will experience a spectacular increase in future decades through an increased use of insecticides and antibiotics.

Students should achieve several basic understandings through a discussion of population growth rates: (1) Underdeveloped nations are confronted with the problem of producing a population structure in which there are too many young people and too few adults for economic efficiency. (2) In most underdeveloped economies, approximately 40 percent of the total population is below 15 years of age. (3) A youthful labor force decreases production on a per capita basis and results in a surplus of unskilled workers. (4) Due to the large proportion of young people, most underdeveloped nations will continue to experience large population increases.

Human Characteristics of Developing Non-Western Cultures

One of the foremost responsibilities of the secondary social studies teacher is to prepare students to live in the global society in which they will live rather than in a world society in which we would like for them to live. The achievement of this objective is dependent upon the teacher's ability to instill within the student an awareness of the nature of the non-Western world. One of the most effective classroom techniques for realizing this goal is to emphasize the human characteristics of non-Western nations. Through such an approach, students can better grasp the significance of cultural differences and achieve the awareness that the vast majority of the world's people are unlike the inhabitants of Western nations in many important respects. By the time a secondary student has completed the study of selected non-Western cultures he should possess an understanding of the following human characteristics:

1. *Most of the world's population is not white.*[54]   Only a cursory examination of the distribution of the world's major ethnic groups by nations and regions and a racial analysis of the global rate of population increase will support this concept entirely.

2. *The majority of the world's people is not Christian.*   Every attempt must be made to make students aware of the significance of religion on a global scale. They must achieve the understanding that other cultures possess different religious beliefs to the same degree that those of the Western world accept the beliefs expounded by Christianity.

3. *Most of the world's population exists on an agrarian subsistence base.*   The major point for student understanding regarding subsistence economies is that the primary human concern is family centered, that is, providing food and clothing for the family on a day-to-day basis. When these circumstances exist, there is little time to give attention to national goals and issues. One of the negative results of subsistence agrarianism on the part of a large segment of a nation's populace is that there exists little nationalism or patriotism, with the consequence that these nations do not possess the national cohesion or viability that characterizes most Western nations.

4. *Most of the world's people live in nations that are experiencing a rapid rate of natural population increase.*   The significance of this situation is exemplified by the problem of improving economic development in the face of rapid population increase. With economic growth in its initial stages in most non-Western nations, just meeting

the basic needs of the increasing population absorbs most of the economic advancement. From the standpoints of economic and social development, therefore, the populations of these nations are a hindrance rather than an asset to national development.

5. *The majority of the populations in most non-Western nations is illiterate in terms of the national language.* As a result of this situation, a high degree of nationalism and patriotism are nearly impossible to develop, since such a large proportion of the population does not comprehend national goals and priorities in terms of the international perspective. Furthermore, nations that are economically backward need a skilled population in most sectors of the economy if they are to achieve any level of technological advancement.

In the secondary social studies curriculum, the predominant strategy for dividing the world for the study of cultural groups is on the basis of "Western and non-Western." A major weakness in such a division is that the cultural differences among the non-Western nations are as great or greater than the difference between the Western and non-Western peoples. These differences are oftentimes overlooked. For instance, when considering non-Western cultures, social studies teachers should emphasize the differences that exist among the Indians, Chinese, Japanese, the Tanzanians, Sudanese, and so on, as well as the differences among the West and non-West.

In addition to the above basic characteristics there are other human elements of non-Western societies of which secondary students should have an understanding. A partial listing of these would include:[55]

1. Low social status for women.
2. Relatively high use of child labor.
3. Uneven distribution of arable land (most productive land in the hands of a very few landlords).
4. Lack of a substantial middle class.
5. Rigid social stratification based upon tradition.
6. A high rate of communicable disease and a general lack of sanitation and medical facilities.
7. Substandard housing conditions.
8. Close interrelationship of the military and government.
9. Very uneven distribution of wealth.
10. Extremely conservative and uneducated populace.

Building a nation in the Western sense of the term is an exceedingly difficult and long task. Whether or not one accepts the prediction that it consists of "an endless round of coups, conquests, revolutions, and wars," it is evident that the so-called "new nations" that have gained independence since World War II have only begun the arduous path to achieving viable and stable national existence.

Conclusion

Throughout the secondary social studies curriculum, there is no more significant relationship than that between man and his natural environment. In the study of nations, highly advanced as well as underdeveloped, the man-land connection is inseparable. Seemingly, however, this association is most obvious in the developing society. The man-land relationship encompasses the total of human features at man's disposal. Students must achieve the awareness that world cultures differ with respect to their control over the environment. A consideration of the general principles of underdevelopment must always include individual exceptions. Students must also understand that the transition from emerging nation to advanced nation tends to be cyclic in many instances. The alleviation of problems in one sector of the economy may result in the creation of equally serious difficulties in other areas. There exists no universal blueprint for achieving high economic status. Economic development for many nations of the world is a long-term prospect and must be understood and appraised accordingly.

ISSUES OF WAR, PEACE, AND REVOLUTION IN WORLD PERSPECTIVE

No international theme is more relevant or of greater significance to secondary social studies instruction than that involving war and peace. Furthermore, it is doubtful that any issue is of more vital concern, in an ultimate context, to the current generation of students. For these reasons it is imperative that secondary teachers provide ample opportunity for the discussion of this vital issue in their social studies classes.

Thermonuclear War

Nuclear war is not inevitable. Regardless of the continuous discussion among the world powers concerning the limiting and restricting of nuclear weapons, the threat of such a holocaust will remain with us for the indefinite future. The United States, the Soviet Union, and the People's Republic of China allocate approximately half their annual budget to sophisticated weapons systems to defend against a possible World War III. In comparison, the annual financial resources invested in means to prevent war and resolve international conflict are relatively minor. This situation, however, is not new to human history. For centuries, most viable nations have invested tremendous financial and human resources in the capabilities to wage war. In global perspective, the military is an old, respected profession; there is no comparable profession concerned with the maintenance of peace.[56]

With regard to discussing the issue of World War III, secondary social studies teachers are confronted with two major tasks in their classroom instruction. First, it is relatively impossible to illustrate or explain to students the tragically gruesome results of a nuclear war. Today's generation of secondary students are far removed from devastation wrought upon the major Japanese and German cities and their populations during World War II. Likewise, the Vietnam conflict of the last decade, barbaric as it was, afforded no opportunity for even a micro-example of what a thermonuclear exchange would involve. Given this situation, the instructor must go to great lengths to gather the best and most meaningful evidence, from the standpoint of student comprehension levels, concerning the significance of a nuclear war before any systematic discussion can take place. The following excerpt, presented by a national authority on thermonuclear war, is an example of the type of hypothesis that should be researched and presented to students prior to any discussion of World War III.

So far as I know, with everything working as well as can be hoped and all foreseeable precautions taken, the most conservative estimates of Americans killed in a major nuclear attack run to about 50 million. We have become callous to gruesome statistics, and this seems at first to be only another gruesome statistic. You think, "Bang!"—and the next morning, if you're still there, you read in the newspapers that 50 million people were killed. But that isn't the way it happens. When we killed close to 200,000 people with those first little old-fashioned uranium bombs that we dropped on Hiroshima and Nagasaki, about the same number of persons were maimed, blinded, burned, poisoned, and otherwise doomed. A lot of them took a long time to die.

That's the way it would be. Not a bang, and a certain number of corpses to bury, but a nation filled with millions of helpless, maimed, tortured, and doomed survivors huddled with their families in shelters, with guns ready to fight off their neighbors, trying to get some uncontaminated food and water.[57]

The second major task confronting secondary social studies teachers in any discussion of World War III involves the problem of attempting to promote student inquiry into the significance of what was referred to by ex-President Eisenhower as the Military-Industrial Complex. Student reflection must not be limited to the situation in the United States but must be considered in global context. Student analysis should be based upon the theme that it would appear impossible to reduce the nuclear arms race among the world powers so long as the contemporary interrelationship exists in these nations between the ever-increasing military establishments and the technological and scientific sectors of the economy. Promoting an objective discussion of this extremely emotional topic will demand the utmost professional skill on the part of the classroom teacher.

Conventional War, Revolution, and Wars of National Liberation

It has been suggested, on the basis of substantial evidence, that today's secondary student will be confronted with some type of war, in the conventional sense, throughout his lifetime. Furthermore, the best evidence indicates that the majority of these conflicts will be comparatively similar in both rationale and strategy to the conflict in Indochina. This thesis is supported by the fact that the more than two-thirds of the world's nations are technologically less-advanced and primarily subsistence societies. Significantly, nearly three-fourths of mankind resides in these nations. In order to initiate economic, social, and political development in these nations, numerous extremist, divisive, and revolutionary groups will become actively involved. As has been the case since World War II among the emerging nations, violence and conflict will undoubtedly continue to erupt on a global scale for the foreseeable future, both in and out of the ideological cold war context existing between East and West.

The responsibilities of the social studies curriculum in this area of concern would appear to be dual in nature. First, every attempt must be made to instill within students the understanding that the "Revolution of Rising Expectations," or the path to political, social, and economic improvement in the underdeveloped world will not be smooth, orderly, and "democratic" in most instances. That the very nature of these socities and what they hope to achieve will result in upheaval in many countries and possibly overt conflict among various traditional and revolutionary groups. Although non-comparable in most instances, some analogies may be drawn between today's revolutions and the combination of forces which led to the American Revolution and the American Civil War.

The second, and perhaps, most significant responsibility of the secondary social studies in the area of conventional war and revolution is that of psychologically preparing today's student to live with the international tension as well as national tension created by these conflicts. They must be prepared to critically examine the policies of the United States toward each individual conflict and they must be able to comprehend the basis for each situation.

CHAPTER 5

Professional Development in Social Studies Education

EVALUATION IN SOCIAL EDUCATION

The difficulties encountered when attempting to develop an objective and valid system for evaluation and grading are among the most frustrating of all the professional problems confronting both the beginning and the experienced secondary social studies teachers. Traditional grading systems are criticized constantly by both professional educators and teachers, but such systems continue to characterize the evaluation of the vast majority of students both in higher and precollegiate education.

Types and Objectives of Evaluation[1]

There are three primary objectives of evaluation which pertain directly to the secondary social studies curriculum. First, there is the acquisition of numerical or "letter" grades derived from various types of examinations, either written or oral. The type of examination or test, however, greatly influences the grading procedure, although the validity of the examination may be in question. For instance, there is little disagreement among teachers that an objective examination, for example, multiple choice, true-false, fill-in-the-blank, and so on, are by far the simplest from which to extract data for purposes of determining a grade. The only two questions the teacher must resolve through this procedure is whether to grade the students on the basis of the examination or to grade them in terms of each individual student's performance in relation to the performance of the entire class — in essence, to have students compete with the examination or with each other (grading on the curve or scaling grades).

However, the objective examination is based upon absolute or descriptive answers (either correct or incorrect). Herein lies the rationale for the basic criticisms of evaluating students on such a basis, since a constant criticism of the social studies program is that the instructional procedure is absolute rather than relative, that students are directed to memorize data that is briefly retained rather than taught to inquire, reflect, and develop the ability to analyze problems in relative terms.

Extracting data from subjective questions for the purpose of evaluation, however, is much more difficult for the instructor. Regardless of whether the questions are based upon assumptions or hypotheses or whether they are of the discussion type, the absolute percentage measure is not available. Although experience makes the grading of such examinations easier, it is still a most difficult and frustrating task. Most teachers will develop some type of comparative procedure whereby the teacher will evaluate subjective questions on the basis of method approach, and content as developed by a selected number of better students in the class.

A second major purpose of evaluation or grading is the attempt to measure student progress.[2] The basic premise here is that students will be motivated to make progress as a result of various evaluation procedures. The results of an examination over a particular topic of study should help the student to improve his performance in his social studies class by better understanding his strengths and weaknesses in that particular area. However, a major concern confronting the instructor is that the student may become seriously discouraged by a low grade and rather than attempting to improve his weaknesses and study habits may, in actuality, continue to perform negatively. It is in such instances as this that the ability of the teacher to instill motivation for academic improvement is vital.

A third rationale for student evaluation is for the purpose of improving instruction.[3] If many students with average and high ability and a high degree of motivation continue to perform poorly on examinations, there is a good indication that something is wrong with either the test construction, classroom instruction, or both. The construction of valid examinations has always been one of the major challenges facing the social studies teacher.

Continuing Problems in Evaluation

The literature in social studies education is full of statements with regard to objectives, goals, and purposes. Currently, a significant proportion of these goals of social studies instruction imply that more attention be given to instilling the skills of inquiry and critical analysis and developing behavioral patterns through emphasis on value and attitudinal formulation.

Unlike testing the mastery of descriptive subject matter, the evaluation of reflective inquiry skills and the acquisition of behavioral objectives is most difficult. There exists a variety of measurement methods that teachers attempt, such as student ability to test hypotheses or assumptions, identify central issues or themes, judge the validity of evidence, and to draw conclusions.[4] Nevertheless, the evaluation of relative objectives will continue to be a priority area for much additional educational research before effective measurement techniques can be designed.

THE PROFESSIONAL EDUCATION OF SECONDARY SOCIAL STUDIES TEACHERS

The education of secondary social studies teachers has traditionally been a subject of great interest and debate. Numerous alternative proposals for implementing change continue to be expressed. The very nature of the social studies curriculum has accounted for the wide divergence of opinion that exists with regard to the preparation of competent secondary teachers.

Divergent Philosophies of Teacher Education

First, there is the widely held position among an influential segment of scholars, professional educators, and teachers that the professional preparation of secondary instructors should consist primarily of vigorous training in preferably one but no more than two of the six or seven social science disciplines comprising the secondary social studies curriculum. One of the foremost arguments expressed in support of this type of education is that the secondary curriculum, unlike the elementary curriculum, should be discipline centered. With an ever-increasing proportion of secondary students entering college and university, it is vital that they be adequately prepared in content to compete in higher education.

The second major school of thought expresses a considerably divergent educational philosophy regarding the preparation of secondary teachers. This group believes that the academic requirements of prospective secondary teachers should encompass a broad range of social science offerings, since the social studies program at the secondary level comprises an integration of data and concepts from all of the academic social science disciplines. Furthermore, this argument continues, the academic training must be broad, since the instructor in secondary education is primarily a practitioner rather than a scholar or specialist. Thus, the secondary teacher must be acquainted with the nature and method of several of the social sciences rather than concentrate on one or two disciplines. In addition, he must be well-grounded in the psychology of learning and have an adequate understanding of education philosophy and the fundamental goals and objectives of social education in a democracy. In essence, the secondary teacher must have a well balanced background consisting of broad exposure to most of the social science disciplines and those elements of professional education which are applicable to secondary education. Success in secondary teaching is not probable if one or the other areas of preparation is deficient.

Basic Components of Teacher-Education Programs[5]

Even though the debate over what constitutes the best professional strategy for the education of secondary social studies teachers will continue as long as the social studies curriculum exists, the fundamental elements of teacher-education programs are basically established by state governing bodies and national accrediting agencies. Since the inception of the contemporary social studies curriculum as endorsed in 1916 by the Committee on Social Studies, appointed by the National Education Association, the teacher-education program for secondary instructors has been stable in the following respects:

1. *General Education.* The rationale for this segment of a prospective teacher's education is that of providing a general background in the areas of world affairs, culture, the humanities, skills of written and oral communication, and additional academic elements that will provide the basis for a liberal education. The prospective social studies teacher should develop a basic knowledge and appreciation of such specific fields as language, literature, music, art, science, mathematics, and the social sciences. Specifically, the standards for accreditation adopted by the National Council for Accreditation of Teacher Education (NCATE) recommend ". . . that at least one-third of each curriculum for prospective teachers consist of studies in the symbolics of information, natural and behavioral sciences, and humanities."

2. *Field of Specialization.* This element consists of the academic areas of learning which will provide the teacher with a fundamental

background in content and method of the social sciences which he will teach at the secondary level—for instance, a specific number of hours from the fields of history, geography, political science, sociology, economics, and so on, which fulfill the accreditation requirements for teaching these subjects in the secondary schools.

3. *Professional Education Sequence.* This element consists of those professional aspects of the teacher-education program such as curriculum planning, educational philosophy, the history of the American educational system, and the psychology of learning. This core of subjects is designed to provide the beginning teacher with the philosophical, developmental, and psychological aspects of teaching at the precollegiate level.

4. *The Student Teaching Experience and Special Methods Courses.* This component provides the prospective secondary teacher with the opportunity to gain competency in the instructional methodology and techniques of teaching the social studies as well as a supervised teaching experience in a secondary classroom.[6]

Student Teaching and Special Methods for Social Studies Teachers

The special methods course and the student teaching experience represent the culmination of both the academic and the professional components of the teacher education program.

One of the most valuable realizations to be achieved through student teaching is an awareness of the semantic haziness concerning the thinking process. In the professional literature, thinking is treated as a total process encompassing everything that goes on in the mind, from daydreaming to creating a concept about cybernetics. Even the most prominent educators and psychologists have failed to distinguish between (1) the elements of thinking or the basic skills of which thinking or the basic skills of which thinking is composed and (2) the strategies of thought, such as inquiry or problem-solving, let alone effectively merging the elements and strategies of the thought process with the selection and presentation of subject matter. Styles of thinking such as convergent and divergent thinking, productive thinking, and critical thinking are expounded simultaneously with fundamental processes such as concept formation, inferring, and generalizing.

This vagueness has resulted in enormous confusion which the student teacher must immediately begin to interpret. He must realize that there exists no systematic or structured formula for content selection, defining relevant or irrelevant content, or implementing the skills of critical inquiry. This situation, however, should not be interpreted negatively. Indeed, the relativity involved in the selection of subject matter and the opportunity to introduce innovative instructional procedures are thoroughly positive aspects of social studies teaching in that they encourage individualism and experimentation on the part of the teacher. There is widespread agreement that the ultimate objectives of social studies instruction are threefold: (1) to instill within students the skills and abilities vital to the decision-making process, (2) to motivate a desire for continued learning throughout the student's lifetime, and (3) to prepare students to function productively in a complex and ever-changing national and global society. How to accomplish these objectives most effectively represents both the challenge and reward of teaching the social studies. An appreciation of the role of the cooperating social studies instructor in his continual effort to realize these goals should be a result of the student teaching experience. On the other hand, if the individual concludes his internship period confident that he has discovered "how to teach," the student teaching experience might well be judged a failure.

The student teaching experience should not be viewed as the conclusion of a prospective teacher's professional education. Rather, it must be considered as the beginning. It is an internship period which should culminate in a combined feeling of confusion, inadequacy, insecurity, and humility with regard to the individual's academic competency, his knowledge of the teacher-learning process, and his understanding of the ultimate purpose of social education in a democratic society.

There is little doubt that social science majors could be better equipped to undertake their student teaching experience in terms of both subject matter preparation and cognizance of instructional techniques. Regarding the latter, criticism of the social studies methods course continues to be universal among pre-service and in-service teachers. It would seem, however, that the answer is not to delete the methods course but to improve it. Traditionally, the coverage in methods courses has been limited literally to teaching "methods," while the academic offerings in the social sciences have and will continue to deal entirely with "content." This polarization of pedagogical sterility within subject matter courses and academic sterility within methods courses has resulted in a most apparent void in the professional preparation of student teachers in the social sciences. Obviously, the preparation of prospective social studies teachers cannot consist of a series of three or four "special methods" courses, for example, a methods course in economics taught by an economist, a methods course in history offered by a historian, or a methods course in civics and government taught by a political scientist. However, it would appear feasible that the professional training of student teachers in the social sciences could be strengthened substantially by designing one basic methods course comprising the social science disciplines and utilizing a "team teaching" approach which would involve several instructors with competency both in the specific academic areas and in modern instructional strategies as well as practical classroom experience in the processes of content translation at the secondary level. The development of a "substantive methods" course, in which content and methodology are complementary and, thus, synonymous, remains one of the foremost tasks confronting social scientists and social studies teachers.

Concerning the relevant nature of subject matter in social studies instruction, student teachers should be aware that content emphasis is, philosophically speaking, a cyclic phenomenon, and relative within itself. For instance, since the inception of the existing secondary social studies curriculum during the second decade of the present century, both content emphasis and pedagogical technique twice have come full-circle, and are presently in the midst of a third cycle. Specifically in terms of scope, the secondary social studies curriculum has alternated from a national – to international – to national content stress and from a non-directive – directive – non-directive methodological rationale in less than 50 years. Similarly, curriculum planners twice have witnessed a reversal of content sequence from a traditional to a contemporary emphasis during the same period. It is vital for prospective social science teachers to understand that what appears to be highly relevant content for today's secondary student won't necessarily constitute relevant subject matter for tomorrow's student or be synonymous with the social issues confronting these students as adults.

The human condition is in a constant and rapid state of change. The study of the past, the mastery of selected background knowledge, and the application of the results of such study in thinking about the present and future is crucially important for students and teachers living in an age of transition. Study of the past may alternatively be used to divert and confuse the students in their thinking about the major issues of their own historical period. A major challenge for the student teacher is to begin the process of identification and selection of what is valid use and what is abuse of the past for the social education of today's students.

Notes

CHAPTER 1

1. Edith West, "The Social Science Disciplines," cited in John M. Ball, John E. Steinbrink, and Joseph P. Stoltman, editors, *The Social Sciences and Geographic Education: A Reader* (New York: John Wiley & Sons, Inc., 1971), p. 281.

2. *Ibid.*, p. 282.

3. *Ibid.*, p. 289.

4. *Ibid.*, pp. 289-92.

5. *Ibid.*, pp. 292-94.

6. Morris R. Lewenstein, *Teaching Social Studies in Junior and Senior High Schools* (Chicago: Rand McNally & Co., 1963), p. 6.

7. Jonathan C. McLendon, *Social Studies in Secondary Education* (New York: The Macmillan Company, 1965), pp. 67-68.

8. Ruth Benedict, "Transmitting Our Democratic Heritage in the Schools," cited in Edwin Fenton, *Teaching the New Social Studies in Secondary Schools* (New York: Holt, Rinehart, & Winston, Inc., 1966), p. 64.

9. Lewenstein, *op, cit.*, pp. 50-51.

10. *Ibid.*

11. *Ibid.*, p. 51.

12. *Ibid.*

13. Henry Steele Commager, "Is Freedom Dying in America," *Look*, Vol. 34, No. 14 (July 14, 1970), pp. 19-20.

14. A thorough discussion of educational objectives for social education is discussed in Benjamin S. Bloom and David R. Krathwohl, "Educational Objectives and Curriculum Development," cited in Edwin Fenton, *op, cit.*, pp. 20-21.

15. Edwin Fenton, *Teaching the New Social Studies in Secondary Schools*, pp. 40-50, *passim.*

16. *Ibid.*, pp. 20-29, *passim.*

17. *Ibid.*, p. 19.

18. One of the most scholarly statements concerning behavioral objectives in the secondary social studies has been presented by C. Benjamin Cox, "Behavior as Objective in Education," *Social Education*, Vol. 35, No. 5 (May, 1971), pp. 435-38.

19. *Ibid.*, pp. 440-41.
20. *Ibid.*, p. 442.

CHAPTER 2

1. A concise review of both the rationale for simulation in the secondary social studies and the characteristics of different simulation games is presented by Norris Sanders, "Changing Strategies of Instruction: Three Case Examples," cited in *Social Studies Curriculum Development: Prospects and Problems*, 39th Yearbook, National Council for the Social Studies, Chapter 5.

2. Edith West, "The Social Science Disciplines," cited in John M. Ball, John E. Steinbrink, and Joseph P. Stoltman, eds., *The Social Sciences and Geographic Education: A Reader* (New York: John Wiley & Sons, Inc., 1971), p. 289.

3. *Ibid.*

4. Morris R. Lewenstein, *Teaching Social Studies in Junior and Senior High Schools* (Chicago: Rand McNally & Co., 1963), pp. 280-81.

5. *Ibid.*, pp. 281-82.

6. Jonathan C. McLendon, *Social Studies in Secondary Education* (New York: The Macmillan Company, 1965), pp. 212-13.

7. *Ibid.*, p. 213.

8. An excellent discussion of interdisciplinary area-studies programs is contained in John M. Thompson, "Area Studies in American Education," cited in *International Dimensions in the Social Studies*, James M. Becker and Howard D. Mehlinger, eds., 38th Yearbook, National Council for the Social Studies, 1968, pp. 145-46.

9. *Ibid.*, p. 146.

CHAPTER 3

1. Mario D. Fantini, "Urban School Reform: Educational Agenda for Tomorrow's America," *Current History*, Vol. 59, No. 351 (November, 1970), p. 267.

2. *Ibid.*

3. *Ibid.*

4. Morris R. Lewenstein, *Teaching Social Studies in Junior and Senior High Schools* (Chicago: Rand McNally & Co.), pp. 42-43.

5. One of the most comprehensive statements concerning the teaching of religion in the public schools has been presented recently by James V. Panoch and David L. Barr, "Should We Teach About Religions in Our Public Schools?" *Social Education*, Vol. 33, No. 8 (December, 1969), pp. 910-13.

6. *Religion in the Public Schools* (New York: Harper & Row, 1964), p. 56, cited in Panoch and Barr, "Should We Teach About Religions in Our Public Schools?", *Social Education*, Vol. 33, No. 8 (December, 1969), p. 910.

7. *Ibid.*

8. *Ibid.* p. 911.

9. *Ibid.* p. 910.

10. *Social Education*, Vol. 33, No. 8 (December, 1969), pp. 917-22.

11. An excellent discussion of this highly controversial topic is found in Louis J. Karmel, "Sex Education No! Sex Education Yes!" *Phi Delta Kappan*, Vol. 52, No. 2 (October, 1970), pp. 95-96.

12. Robert C. Weaver, "Rebuilding American Cities: An Overview," *Current History*, Vol. 55, No. 328 (December, 1968), p. 321.

13. Population Bulletin (Washington, D.C.: Population Reference Bureau, Inc., December, 1970), pp. 4-5.

14. *Population Bulletin* (Washington, D.C.: Population Reference Bureau, Inc., December, 1970), p. 8.

15. Fantini, *op, cit.*, p. 267.

16. Peter Lupsha, "The Politics of Urban Change," *Current History*, Vol. 55, No. 328 (December, 1968), p. 329.

17. Yetta M. Goodman, "Metropolitan Man and the Social Studies," *Social Education*, Vol. 33, No. 6 (October, 1969), p. 700.

18. *Ibid.*

19. *Ibid.*, p. 701.

20. *Ibid.*, p. 702.

21. Hubert E. Kirkland, "Teaching Urban Realities in Primary Classrooms," *Social Education*, Vol. 33, No. 6 (October, 1969), pp. 703-04.

22. Lloyd M. Jones, "Teaching About Urban Life in the Middle Grades," *Social Education*, Vol. 33, No. 6 (October, 1969), p. 705.

23. James F. Richardson, "The Historical Roots of Our Urban Crises," *Current History*, Vol. 59, No. 351 (November, 1970), p. 257.

24. *Ibid.*, p. 259.

25. Luther Gulick, "The Financial Plight of the Cities," *Current History*, Vol. 55, No. 328 (December, 1968), p. 337.

26. One of the most enlightening statements reflecting the difficulties of implementing "Black Studies" programs is contained in Roger A. Fischer, "Ghetto and Gown: The Birth of Black Studies," *Current History*, Vol. 57, No. 339 (November, 1969), pp. 290-99.

27. A significant portion of this section was taken from an excellent review by A. Harry Passow, "Urban Public School Systems," *Current History*, Vol. 55, No. 328 (December, 1968), pp. 346-51.

28. Marston Bates, "The Human Ecosystem," *Resources and Man*, National Academy of Sciences (San Francisco: W. H. Freeman & Co., 1969), p. 21.

29. *Population Bulletin* (Washington, D.C.: Population Reference Bureau, Inc., December, 1970), p. 11.

30. *Population Bulletin* (Washington, D.C.: Population Reference Bureau, Inc., June, 1970), p. 3.

31. *Ibid.*, p. 4.

32. *Ibid.*

33. In 1798 the British social economist, Thomas Malthus, published a book entitled, *An Essay on the Principle of Population as It Affects the Future Improvement of Mankind.* His basic theory was that population increases faster than the means of subsistence and, therefore, must be controlled either by checking the rate of reproduction or by maintaining high death rates.

34. *Population Bulletin,* December, 1970, *op. cit.,* p. 9.

35. *Ibid.*

36. *Ibid.,* pp. 12-13.

37. *Ibid.*

38. Paul R. Ehrlich and Anne H. Ehrlich, *Population, Resources, Environment: Issues In Human Ecology* (San Francisco: W. H. Freeman & Co., 1970), p. 259.

39. *Ibid.*

40. Harrison Brown, "After the Population Explosion," *Saturday Review* (June 26, 1971), p. 12.

41. *Ibid.*

42. *Ibid.*

CHAPTER 4

1. Numerous current global population statistics are presented in each monthly issue of the *Population Bulletin* (Washington, D.C.: Population Reference Bureau, Inc.).

2. A prediction of global population trends for several centuries in the future is presented in Emrys Jones, *Human Geography* (New York: Frederick A. Praeger, Publishers, 1966), pp. 19-30.

3. Global demographic projections for the remainder of the twentieth century are contained in *Population Bulletin* (Washington, D.C.: Population Reference Bureau, Inc., October, 1965), pp. 83-91.

4. *Ibid.,* pp. 84-85.

5. *Population Bulletin,* 1965, *op. cit.,* pp. 88-90.

6. *Population Reference Bureau Press Release* (Washington, D.C.: Population Reference Bureau, Inc., April, 1969), pp. 1-4.

7. *Population Bulletin* (October, 1965), *op. cit.,* p. 76.

8. Arthur H. Doerr, *An Introduction to Economic Geography* (Dubuque, Iowa: Wm. C. Brown Company, Publishers, 1969), p. 7.

9. William and Paul Paddock, "Famine — 1975!" Cited in *Can Mass Starvation Be Prevented?,* Report No. 7 (New York: International Planned Parenthood Federation, Fall, 1967), p. 7.

10. A brief but current interpretation of Malthusian doctrine is presented in Rhoads Murphy, *The Scope of Geography* (Chicago: Rand McNally & Co., 1969), pp. 158-59.

11. Chiao-Min Hsieh, *China: Ageless Land and Countless People* (Princeton, New Jersey: D. Van Nostrand Company, Inc., 1967), p. 111.

12. A concise review of the current Roman Catholic position toward artificial birth control techniques is presented in *Population Profile* (Washington, D.C.: Population Reference Bureau, Inc., July, 1968), pp. 5-7.

13. Jan O. M. Broek and John W. Webb, *A Geography of Mankind* (New York: McGraw-Hill Book Company, 1968), p. 483.

14. Arthur H. Doerr, *op. cit.,* pp. 11-15.

15. *Population Bulletin* (Washington, D.C.: Population Reference Bureau, Inc., March, 1969), p. 43.

16. Population Reference Bureau Press Release, *op. cit.*, p. 3.

17. Frank W. Notestein, "The Population Crises: Reasons for Hope," *Foreign Affairs* (October, 1967), p. 170.

18. Alvin Z. Rubinstein, ed., *The Foreign Policy of the Soviet Union* (New York: Random House, 1960), p. 6.

19. Two brief but excellent reviews of Marxist-Leninist ideology for secondary social studies teachers are presented in Andrew Gyorgy, *Communism in Perspective* (Boston: Allyn & Bacon, Inc., 1965), pp. 21-30, and Alvin Z. Rubinstein, *op, cit.*, pp. 4-13.

20. *New York Times,* May 31, 1969.

21. George Lichtheim, "What Is Left of Communism?" *Foreign Affairs* (October, 1967), pp. 78-87, *passim.*

22. *Ibid.*

23. A practical discussion of both the positive and negative aspects of central economic planning for secondary social studies instructors is contained in Marshall I. Goldman, "The Soviet Economy," *Current History* (November, 1968), pp. 288-92.

24. Harry G. Shaffer, ed., *The Soviet System in Theory and Practice* (New York: Appleton-Century-Crofts, 1965), pp. 145-46.

25. George N. Halm, "Fundamental Principles of Central Planning in the U.S.S.R.," cited in Harry G. Shaffer, *ibid.*, pp. 147-48.

26. Alvin Z. Rubinstein, *et al., Communist Political Systems* (Englewood Cliffs, New Jersey: Prentice-Hall, Inc., 1966), pp. 228-33.

27. *Ibid.*, p. 197.

28. *Ibid.*, p. 201.

29. *Ibid.*

30. Robert J. Havighurst, *Comparative Perspectives on Education* (Boston: Little, Brown & Co., 1968), pp. 58-61, 114-18.

31. *Ibid.*

32. Andrew Gyorgy, *op. cit.*, pp. 165-70.

33. C. T. Hu, "Target of the Cultural Revolution," *Saturday Review* (August 19, 1967), pp. 52-54.

34. This appraisal is based upon personal observations of the writer in the Soviet Union and eastern Europe, summer 1964, East Germany and East Berlin, 1968, 1969, and the Soviet Union, winter, 1970.

35. Based upon personal conversations with Soviet and east European nationals, 1969-70.

36. D. W. Fryer, *World Economic Development* (New York: McGraw-Hill Book Company, 1965), p. 18.

37. Excellent appraisals of national economic development within Africa and Latin America are presented in William A. Hance, *The Geography of Modern Africa* (New York: Columbia University Press, 1964). Also Preston E. James, *Latin America,* 3rd ed. (New York: The Odyssey Press, 1959).

38. D. W. Fryer, *op, cit.*, pp. 13-21.

39. Preston James, *op, cit.*, p. 11.

40. John P. Augelli, "Brasilia: The Emergence of a National Capital," *Journal of Geography,* Vol. 62 (1963), p. 242.

41. Allen K. Philbrick, *This Human World* (New York: John Wiley & Sons, 1963), p. 201.

42. For a thorough discussion of this topic, see Lewis M. Alexander, *World Political Patterns* (Chicago: Rand McNally & Co., 1963), pp. 194-203.

43. W. A. Douglas Jackson, *Russo-Chinese Borderlands* (Princeton: D. Van Nostrand Company, 1962), pp. 89-91.

44. Many of the more recently published school atlases include a rural/urban ratio for individual nations.

45. United Nations, Economic and Social Council, *Preliminary Study of the Demographic Situation in Latin America* (April, 1961), p. 87.

46. Paul E. Lydolph, *Geography of the U.S.S.R.* (New York: John Wiley & Sons, 1964), p. 261.

47. An excellent source for reviewing the nature and functions of different types of regions is Rhoads Murphey, *An Introduction to Geography* (Chicago: Rand McNally & Co., 1963), pp. 44-51.

48. See Howard F. Cline, *Mexico: Revolution to Evolution* (New York: Oxford University Press, 1963), pp. 52-53.

49. For a detailed discussion of agrarian problems in Africa and Latin America, see W. S. Rycroft and M. M. Clemmer, *A Factual Study of Africa* and *A Factual Study of Latin America* (New York: Commission on Ecumenical Missions and Relations, The United Presbyterian Church in the U.S.A., 1963).

50. Although the proportionate figures vary considerably in different areas, the great disparity in land tenure is one of the most obvious phenomena in the pre-industrial economy.

51. For instance, in 16 of the Latin American countries, the first city contains approximately four times the population of the second largest city.

52. Jack Woddis, *Africa—The Roots of Revolt* (New York: The Citadel Press, 1960), pp. 129-31.

53. Population Reference Bureau, *op. cit.*, p. 167.

54. An excellent detailed discussion of many of the societal characteristics of non-Western cultures has been recently presented by David E. Christensen, "Two-Thirds of the World," *Social Education*, Vol. 31, No. 3 (March, 1967), pp. 212-17.

55. Don Adams and Robert M. Bjork, *Education in Developing Areas* (New York: David McKay Company, Inc., 1969), pp. 5-6.

56. Quincy Wright, William M. Evan, and Morton Deutsch, *Presenting World War III* (New York: Simon & Schuster, 1962), p. 9.

57. George Wald, "Man's Concern Must Be Life, Not Death" (Washington, D.C.: Population Reference Bureau, Selection No. 27, April, 1969), p. 4.

CHAPTER 5

1. An excellent reference dealing with the problems of grading and evaluation for secondary social studies teachers is Dana G. Kurfman, "Evaluating Geography Learning," cited in Phillip Bacon, ed., *Focus on Geography*, 40th Yearbook (Washington, D.C.: National Council for the Social Studies, 1970), pp. 355-77.

2. Fred T. Wilhelms, ed., *Evaluation as Feedback and Guide* (Washington, D.C.: Association for Supervision and Curriculum Development, 1967), cited in Dana G. Kurfman, "Evaluating Geographic Learning," pp. 357-58.

3. *Ibid.*, p. 358.

4. One of the most beneficial statements concerning the evaluation of inquiry-oriented and reflective thought has been presented recently by Dana Kurfman, "The Evaluation of Effective Thinking," cited in Jean Fair and Fannie R. Shaftel, eds., *Effective Thinking in the Social Studies*, 37th Yearbook (Washington, D.C.: National Council for the Social Studies, 1967), pp. 233-38.

5. A recent position paper concerning the academic and professional standards for both elementary and secondary social studies teachers, as defined by the National Council for the Social Studies, is contained in *Social Education*, Vol. 35, No. 8 (December, 1971), pp. 847-52.

6. John Jarolimek, "The Preparation of Geography Teachers," *Focus on Geography*, 40th Yearbook (Washington, D.C.: National Council for the Social Studies, 1970), pp. 425-32.

Selected Bibliography

BACON, PHILLIP (ed.). *Focus on Geography: Key Concepts and Teaching Strategies*, 40th Yearbook. Washington, D.C.: National Council for the Social Studies, 1970.

BALL, JOHN M., JOHN E. STEINBRINK, and JOSEPH P. STOLTMAN (eds.). *The Social Sciences and Geographic Education*. New York: John Wiley & Sons, Inc., 1971.

BECKER, JAMES M., and HOWARD D. MEHLINGER (eds.). *International Dimensions in the Social Studies*, 38th Yearbook. Washington, D.C.: National Council for the Social Studies, 1968.

EHRLICH, PAUL R., and ANNE H. EHRLICH. *Population, Resources, Environment: Issues in Human Ecology*. San Francisco: W. H. Freeman & Co., 1970.

FAIR, JEAN, and FANNIE R. SHAFTEL (eds.). *Effective Thinking in the Social Studies*, 37th Yearbook. Washington, D.C.: National Council for the Social Studies, 1967.

FELDMAN, MARTIN, and ELI SEIFMAN. *The Social Studies: Structure, Models, and Strategies*. Englewood Cliffs, N.J.: Prentice-Hall, Inc., 1969.

FENTON, EDWIN. *Teaching the New Social Studies in Secondary Schools*. New York: Holt, Rinehart, & Winston, Inc., 1967.

FRASER, DOROTHY McCLURE (ed.). *Social Studies Curriculum Development: Prospects and Problems*, 39th Yearbook. Washington, D.C.: National Council for the Social Studies, 1969.

GARVEY, DALE M. "Simulation: A Catalogue of Judgements, Findings, and Hunches," in *Educational Aspects of Simulation*, ed. by P. J. TANSEY. London: McGraw-Hill Book Company, 1971. Chapter 9.

HANNA, PAUL R., ROSE E. SABAROFF, GORDON F. DAVIES, and CHARLES R. FARRAR. *Geography in the Teaching of Social Studies*. Boston: Houghton Mifflin Co., 1966.

LEWENSTEIN, MORRIS R. *Teaching Social Studies in Junior and Senior High Schools*. Chicago: Rand McNally & Co., 1963.

McLENDON, JONATHON C. *Social Studies in Secondary Education*. New York: The Macmillan Co., 1965.

MAGER, ROBERT F. *Preparing Instructional Objectives*. Palo Alto, Calif.: Fearon Publishers, 1962.

113

MASSIALAS, BYRON G., and C. BENJAMIN COX. *Inquiry in Social Studies.* New York: McGraw-Hill Co., 1966.

METCALF, LAWRENCE E. (ed.). *Values Education: Rationale, Strategies, and Procedures,* 41st Yearbook. Washington, D.C.: National Council for the Social Studies, 1971.

MORRIS, JOHN W. (ed.). *Methods of Geographic Instruction.* Waltham, Mass.: Blaisdell Publishing Co., 1968.

NATIONAL ACADEMY OF SCIENCES. *Resources and Man.* San Francisco: W. H. Freeman & Co., 1969.

ROBINSON, DONALD W. *Promising Practices in Civic Education.* Washington, D.C.: National Council for the Social Studies, 1967.